Mastering Linux Shell Scripting

Master the complexities of Bash shell scripting and unlock the power of shell for your enterprise

Andrew Mallett

BIRMINGHAM - MUMBAI

Mastering Linux Shell Scripting

First published: December 2015

Production reference: 1171215

Published by Packt Publishing Ltd.
Livery Place
35 Livery Street
Birmingham B3 2PB, UK.

ISBN 978-1-78439-697-8

www.packtpub.com

Credits

Author
Andrew Mallett

Reviewer
Peter Ducai

Commissioning Editor
Kartikey Pandey

Acquisition Editors
Kirk D'costa

Harsha Bharwani

Content Development Editor
Mayur Pawanikar

Technical Editor
Saurabh Malhotra

Copy Editor
Sneha Singh

Project Coordinator
Nidhi Joshi

Proofreader
Safis Editing

Indexer
Hemangini Bari

Production Coordinator
Shantanu N. Zagade

Cover Work
Shantanu N. Zagade

About the Author

Andrew Mallett is the owner of The Urban Penguin and is a comprehensive provider for professional Linux software development, training, and services. Having always been a command-line fan, he feels that so much time can be saved through knowing command-line shortcuts and scripting. TheUrbanPenguin YouTube channel, maintained by Andrew, has well over 800 videos to support this and he has authored four other Packt titles.

About the Reviewer

Peter Ducai has worked for more than 15 years within the IT industry, which includes programming in C, Java, Python, administration, and troubleshooting OS (mainly Unix/Linux), and also testing and automation.

Currently working as a contractor for HP, he specializes in network automation.

He has worked on the book, *Learning Embedded Linux Using the Yocto Project*.

I want to thank Becca for making my busy life easier.

www.PacktPub.com

Support files, eBooks, discount offers, and more

For support files and downloads related to your book, please visit www.PacktPub.com.

Did you know that Packt offers eBook versions of every book published, with PDF and ePub files available? You can upgrade to the eBook version at www.PacktPub.com and as a print book customer, you are entitled to a discount on the eBook copy. Get in touch with us at service@packtpub.com for more details.

At www.PacktPub.com, you can also read a collection of free technical articles, sign up for a range of free newsletters and receive exclusive discounts and offers on Packt books and eBooks.

https://www2.packtpub.com/books/subscription/packtlib

Do you need instant solutions to your IT questions? PacktLib is Packt's online digital book library. Here, you can search, access, and read Packt's entire library of books.

Why subscribe?

- Fully searchable across every book published by Packt
- Copy and paste, print, and bookmark content
- On demand and accessible via a web browser

Free access for Packt account holders

If you have an account with Packt at www.PacktPub.com, you can use this to access PacktLib today and view 9 entirely free books. Simply use your login credentials for immediate access.

Table of Contents

Preface

Mastering Linux Shell Scripting will become your Bible and a handbook to create and edit bash shell scripts in Linux, OS X, or Unix. Starting with the fundamentals, we quickly move onto helping you create useful scripts with practical examples. In this way, your learning becomes effective and quick. With each chapter, we provide explanations of the code and code examples, so from a learning book this becomes a book that you can use as a ready reference, if you need to understand how to program a specific task.

What this book covers

Chapter 1, What and Why of Scripting with Bash, explains how to create and name scripts. Once you have the script created you can make it executable and welcome yourself to the world. If you have little or no knowledge of scripting then you can start here.

Chapter 2, Creating Interactive Scripts, covers the scripts we will need to work in a more flexible manner and accept arguments or even prompt the user for input during the script execution. I am sure that you have seen scripts similar to this asking for installation directories or server's tp connect to.

Chapter 3, Conditions Attached, covers the use of keywords, such as "if", and commands like "test". It tells us how we can start creating decision structures in the code and then prompt the user for input, if we have not provided arguments; otherwise, we can
run silently.

Chapter 4, Creating Code Snippets, covers the vim text editor, which is very powerful and also syntax highlighting to help us edit the script. However, we can also read into files of the current script. In this way, we can create snippets of code to represent commonly used blocks.

Chapter 5, Alternative Syntax, tells us how we can abbreviate the test command to just a single [, we can also use [[and ((depending on your needs.

Chapter 6, Iterating with Loops, covers how loops are also conditional statements. We can repeat a block of code while a condition is true or false. In this way, using for, while, or until we can have the script complete the repetitive code sequences.

Chapter 7, Creating Building Blocks with Functions, covers how functions can encapsulate the code that we need to repeat within the script. This can help with readability and how easy a script is to maintain.

Chapter 8, Introducing sed, the stream editor, tells us how sed can be used to edit files dynamically and implement it in scripts. In this chapter, we look at how to use and work with sed.

Chapter 9, Automating Apache Virtual Hosts, covers the practical recipes that we can take away when we create a script to create virtual hosts on an Apache HTTPD server. We use sed within the scripts to edit the template used to define virtual hosts.

Chapter 10, Awk Fundamentals, looks at how we can start to process text date from the command line and using awk is another very powerful tool in Linux.

Chapter 11, Summarizing Logs with Awk, tells us about the first practical example we look at with awk, allowing us to process log files on the web server. It also looks at how to report the IP address that has access to the server most often, as well as, how many errors occur and of which type.

Chapter 12, A Better lastlog with Awk, looks at more examples that we can use in awk to filter and format data provided by the lastlog command. It drills down to the specific information that we want and removes information we do not need.

Chapter 13, Using Perl as a Bash Scripting Alternative, introduces the Perl scripting language and the advantages that it can offer. We are not restricted to just using bash we also have Perl as a scripting language.

Chapter 14, Using Python as a Bash Scripting Alternative, introduces you to Python and the Zen of Python that will help you with all programming languages. Like Perl, Python is a scripting language that can extend the functionality of your scripts.

What you need for this book

Using any Linux distribution with the bash shell should be sufficient to complete this book. In the book we use examples that are produced using the Raspbian distribution on a Raspberry Pi; however, Linux distribution should be sufficient. If you have access to the command line in OS X on Apple systems, then you should be able to carry out most of the exercises without Linux.

Who this book is for

Mastering Linux Shell Scripting has been written for Linux administrators who want to automate tasks in their daily lives, saving time and effort. You need to have command-line experience and be familiar with the tasks that you need to automate. A basic knowledge of scripting is expected.

Conventions

In this book, you will find a number of text styles that distinguish between different kinds of information. Here are some examples of these styles and an explanation of their meaning.

Code words in text, database table names, folder names, filenames, file extensions, pathnames, dummy URLs, user input, and Twitter handles are shown as follows: "We again see that the basename is evaluated first, but we do not see the more detailed steps involved in running that command."

A block of code is set as follows:

```
#!/bin/bash
echo "You are using $0"
echo "Hello $*"
exit 0
```

When we wish to draw your attention to a particular part of a code block, the relevant lines or items are set in bold:

```
#!/bin/bash
echo "You are using $0"
echo "Hello $*"
exit 0
```

Any command-line input or output is written as follows:

```
$ bash -x $HOME/bin/hello2.sh fred
```

New terms and **important words** are shown in bold. Words that you see on the screen, for example, in menus or dialog boxes, appear in the text like this: "Clicking the **Next** button moves you to the next screen."

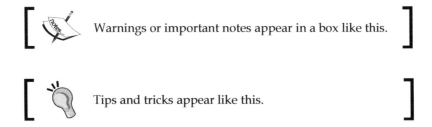

Warnings or important notes appear in a box like this.

Tips and tricks appear like this.

Reader feedback

Feedback from our readers is always welcome. Let us know what you think about this book—what you liked or disliked. Reader feedback is important for us as it helps us develop titles that you will really get the most out of.

To send us general feedback, simply e-mail feedback@packtpub.com, and mention the book's title in the subject of your message.

If there is a topic that you have expertise in and you are interested in either writing or contributing to a book, see our author guide at www.packtpub.com/authors.

Customer support

Now that you are the proud owner of a Packt book, we have a number of things to help you to get the most from your purchase.

Downloading the example code

You can download the example code files from your account at http://www.packtpub.com for all the Packt Publishing books you have purchased. If you purchased this book elsewhere, you can visit http://www.packtpub.com/support and register to have the files e-mailed directly to you.

Downloading the color images of this book

We also provide you with a PDF file that has color images of the screenshots/ diagrams used in this book. The color images will help you better understand the changes in the output. You can download this file from: `http://www.packtpub. com/sites/default/files/downloads/MasteringLinuxShellScripting_ ColorImages.pdf`.

Errata

Although we have taken every care to ensure the accuracy of our content, mistakes do happen. If you find a mistake in one of our books—maybe a mistake in the text or the code—we would be grateful if you could report this to us. By doing so, you can save other readers from frustration and help us improve subsequent versions of this book. If you find any errata, please report them by visiting `http://www.packtpub. com/submit-errata`, selecting your book, clicking on the **Errata Submission Form** link, and entering the details of your errata. Once your errata are verified, your submission will be accepted and the errata will be uploaded to our website or added to any list of existing errata under the Errata section of that title.

To view the previously submitted errata, go to `https://www.packtpub.com/books/ content/support` and enter the name of the book in the search field. The required information will appear under the **Errata** section.

Piracy

Piracy of copyrighted material on the Internet is an ongoing problem across all media. At Packt, we take the protection of our copyright and licenses very seriously. If you come across any illegal copies of our works in any form on the Internet, please provide us with the location address or website name immediately so that we can pursue a remedy.

Please contact us at `copyright@packtpub.com` with a link to the suspected pirated material.

We appreciate your help in protecting our authors and our ability to bring you valuable content.

Questions

If you have a problem with any aspect of this book, you can contact us at `questions@packtpub.com`, and we will do our best to address the problem.

1
What and Why of Scripting with Bash

Welcome to the what and why of bash scripting. My name is Andrew Mallett and I am a bash scripting junkie or perhaps more accurately: a scripting junkie. As an administrator, I fail to see the need to do repetitive tasks manually. We get time for more interesting things when we choose scripts to carry out the laborious tasks that we don't like. In this chapter, we will introduce you to the what and why of bash scripting. If you are new, it will help you become familiar with scripts and also provide some great insights for those with more experience and who want to improve their skills. As we make our way through the chapter, each element is designed to be added to your knowledge to help you achieve your goals. While doing so, we will be covering the following topics:

- Bash vulnerabilities
- The bash command hierarchy
- Preparing text editors for scripting
- Creating and executing scripts
- Debugging your scripts

Bash vulnerabilities

For this book, I will be working entirely on a Raspberry Pi 2 running Raspbian, a Linux distribution similar to Debian, and Ubuntu; although for you, the operating system you choose to work with is immaterial, in reality, as is the version of bash. The bash version I am using is 4.2.37(1). If you are using the OS X operating system, the default command line environment is **bash**.

To return the operating system being used, type the following command if it is installed:

```
$ lsb_release -a
```

The output from my system is shown in the following screenshot:

```
No LSB modules are available.
Distributor ID: Debian
Description:    Debian GNU/Linux 7.8 (wheezy)
Release:        7.8
Codename:       wheezy
pi@pilabs ~ $
```

The easiest way to determine the version of bash that you are using is to print the value of a variable. The following command will display your bash version:

```
$ echo $BASH_VERSION
```

The following screenshot displays the output from my system:

```
pi@pilabs ~ $ echo $BASH_VERSION
4.2.37(1)-release
pi@pilabs ~ $
```

In 2014, there was a well-publicized bug within bash that had been there for many years — the shell-shock bug. If your system is kept up-to-date, then it is not likely to be an issue but it is worth checking. The bug allows malicious code to be executed from within a malformed function. As a standard user, you can run the following code to test for the vulnerabilities on your system. This code comes from Red Hat and is not malicious but if you are unsure then please seek advice.

The following is the code from Red Hat to test for the vulnerability:

```
$ env 'x=() { :;}; echo vulnerable''BASH_FUNC_x()=() { :;}; echo
vulnerable' bash -c "echo test"
```

If your system is free from this first vulnerability the output should be as shown in the following screenshot:

```
bash: warning: x: ignoring function definition attempt
bash: error importing function definition for `BASH_FUNC_x'
test
```

To test for the last vulnerability from this bug, we can use the following test, which is again from Red Hat:

```
cd /tmp; rm -f /tmp/echo; env 'x=() { (a)=>\' bash -c "echo date"; cat /
tmp/echo
```

The output from a patched version of bash should look like the following screenshot:

```
date
cat: /tmp/echo: No such file or directory
```

If the output from either of these command lines is different, then your system may be vulnerable to shell-shock and I would update bash or at least take further advice from a security professional.

The bash command hierarchy

When working on at the bash shell and when you are sitting comfortably at your prompt eagerly waiting to type a command, you will most likely feel that it is a simple matter of typing and hitting the *Enter* key. You should know better than to think that things are never quite as simple as we imagine.

Command type

For example, if we type and enter `ls` to list files, it will be reasonable to think that we were running the command. It is possible, but we will be running an alias often. Aliases exist in memory as a shortcut to commands or commands with options; these aliases are used before we even check for the file. The bash shell built-in command `type` can come to our aid here. The `type` command will display the type of command for a given word entered at the command line. The types of command is listed as follows:

- Alias
- Function
- Shell built in
- Keyword
- File

This list is also a representative of the order in which they are searched. As we can see, it is not until the very end where we search for the executable file `ls`.

The following command demonstrates the simple use type:

```
$ type ls
ls is aliased to `ls --color=auto'
```

We can extend this further to display all the matches for the given command:

```
$ type -a ls
ls is aliased to `ls --color=auto'
ls is /bin/ls
```

If we need to just type in the output, we can use the -t option. This is useful when we need to test the command type from within a script and only need the type to be returned. This excludes the superfluous information; thus, making it easier for us humans to read. Consider the following command and output:

```
$ type -t ls
alias
```

The output is clear and simple and just what a computer or script requires.

The built-in type can also be used to identify shell keywords such as if, case, function, and so on. The following command shows type being used against multiple arguments and types:

```
$ type ls quote pwd do id
```

The output of the command is shown in the following screenshot:

```
pi@pilabs /tmp $ type ls quote pwd do id
ls is aliased to `ls --color=auto'
quote is a function
quote ()
{
    local quoted=${1//\'/\'\\\'\'};
    printf "'%s'" "$quoted"
}
pwd is a shell builtin
do is a shell keyword
id is /usr/bin/id
pi@pilabs /tmp $ _
```

You can also see that the function definition is printed when we stumble across a function when using type.

Command PATH

Linux will check for executables in the PATH environment only when the full or relative path to the program is supplied. In general, the current directory is not searched unless it is in the PATH. It is possible to include our current directory within the PATH by adding the directory to the PATH variable. This is shown in the following code example:

```
$ export PATH=$PATH:.
```

This appends the current directory to the value of the PATH variable each item the PATH is separated using the colon. Now, your PATH is updated to include the current working directory and each time you change directories, the scripts can be executed easily. In general, organizing scripts into a structured directory hierarchy is probably a great idea. Consider creating a subdirectory called bin within your home directory and add the scripts into that folder. Adding $HOME/bin to your PATH variable will enable you to find the scripts by name and without the file path.

The following command-line list will only create the directory, if it does not already exist:

```
$ test -d $HOME/bin || mkdir $HOME/bin
```

Although the above command-line list is not strictly necessary, it does show that scripting in bash is not limited to the actual script and we can use conditional statements and other syntax directly at the command line. From our viewpoint, we know that the preceding command will work whether you have the bin directory or not. The use of the $HOME variable ensures that the command will work without considering your current file system context.

As we work through the book, we will add scripts into the $HOME/bin directory so that they can be executed regardless of our working directory.

Preparing text editors for scripting

Throughout the book, I will be working on the command line of Raspberry Pi and this will include the creation and editing of the scripts. You, of course, can choose the way you wish to edit your script and may prefer to make use of a graphical editor and I will show some settings in gedit. I will make one excursion to a Red Hat system to show screenshots of gedit in this chapter.

To help make the command line editor easier to use, we can enable options and we can persist with these options through hidden configuration files. The gedit and other GUI editors and their menus will provide similar functionality.

Configuring vim

Editing the command line is often a must and is a part of my everyday life. Setting up common options that make life easier in the editor give us the reliability and consistency you need, a little like scripting itself. We will set some useful options in the vi or vim editor file, $HOME/.vimrc.

The options we set are detailed in the following list:

- **showmode**: Ensures we see when we are in insert mode
- **nohlsearch**: Does not highlight the words that we have searched for
- **autoindent**: We indent our code often; this allows us to return to the last indent level rather than the start of a new line on each carriage return
- **tabstop=4**: Sets a tab to be four spaces
- **expandtab**: Converts tabs to spaces, which is useful when the file moves to other systems
- **syntax on**: Note that this does not use the set command and is used to turn on syntax highlighting

When these options are set, the $HOME/.vimrc file should look similar to this:

```
set showmode nohlsearch
set autoindent tabstop=4
set expandtab
syntax on
```

Configuring nano

The nano text edit is increasing in importance and it is the default editor in many systems. Personally, I don't like the navigation or the lack of navigation features that it has. It can be customized in the same way as vim. This time we will edit the $HOME/.nanorc file. Your edited file should look something like the following:

```
set autoindent
set tabsize 4
include /usr/share/nano/sh.nanorc
```

The last line enables syntax highlighting for shell scripts.

Configuring gedit

Graphical editors, such as gedit, can be configured using the preferences menu and are pretty straight forward.

Enabling tab spacing to be set to **4** spaces and expanding tabs to spaces can be done using the **Preference | Editor** tab, as shown in the following screenshot:

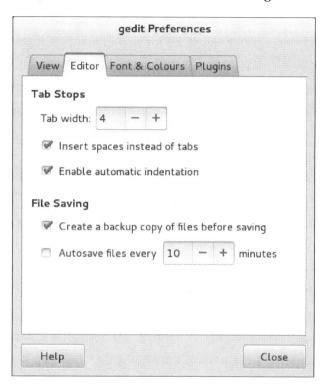

Downloading the example code

You can download the example code files from your account at http://www.packtpub.com for all the Packt Publishing books you have purchased. If you purchased this book elsewhere, you can visit http://www.packtpub.com/support and register to have the files e-mailed directly to you.

Another very useful feature is found on the **Preferences | Plugins** tab. Here, we can enable the **Snippets** plugin that can be used to insert code samples. This is shown in the following screenshot:

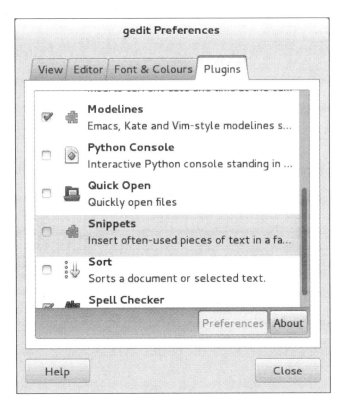

For the rest of the book, we will be working on the command line in and in vim; feel free to use the editor that you work with best. We have now laid the foundations to create good scripts and although whitespace, tabs, and spaces in bash scripts are not significant; a well laid out file with consistent spacing is easy to read. When we look at Python later in the book, you will realize that in some languages the whitespace is significant to the language and it is better to adopt the good habits early.

Creating and executing scripts

With our editors primed and ready, we can now move quickly to creating and executing our scripts. If you are reading this book with some prior experience, I will warn you that we are going to start with the basics but we will also include looking at positional parameters; feel free to move on at your own pace.

Hello World!

As you know, it is almost obligatory to begin with a `hello world` script and we will not disappoint as far as this is concerned. We will begin by creating a new script `$HOME/bin/hello1.sh`. The contents of the file should read as in the following screenshot:

```
#!/bin/bash
echo "Hello World"
exit 0
```

I am hoping that you haven't struggled with this too much; it is just three lines after all. I encourage you to run through the examples as you read to really help you instill the information with a good hands-on practice.

- `#!/bin/bash`: Normally, this is always the first line of the script and is known as the shebang. The shebang starts with a comment but the system still uses this line. A comment in a shell script has the # symbol. The shebang instructs the system to the interpreter to execute the script. We use bash for shell scripts and we may use PHP or Perl for other scripts, as required. If we do not add this line, then the commands will be run within the current shell; it may cause issues if we run another shell.

- `echo "Hello World"`: The `echo` command will be picked up in a built-in shell and can be used to write a standard output, STDOUT, this defaults to the screen. The information to print is enclosed in double-quotes, there will be more on quotes later.

- `exit 0`: The `exit` command is a built in shell and is used to leave or exit the script. The `exit` code is supplied as an integer argument. A value of anything other than 0 will indicate some type of error in the script's execution.

Executing the script

With the script saved in our PATH environment, it still will not execute as a standalone script. We will have to assign and execute permissions for the file, as needed. For a simple test, we can run the file directly with bash. The following command shows you how to do this:

```
$ bash $HOME/bin/hello1.sh
```

We should be rewarded with the `Hello World` text being displayed back on our screens. This is not a long-term solution, as we need to have the script in the $HOME/bin directory, specifically, to make the running of the script easy from any location without typing the full path. We need to add in the execute permissions as shown in the following code:

```
$ chmod +x $HOME/bin/hello1.sh
```

We should now be able to run the script simply, as shown in the following screenshot:

```
pi@pilabs ~ $ chmod +x $HOME/bin/hello1.sh
pi@pilabs ~ $ hello1.sh
Hello World
pi@pilabs ~ $ _
```

Checking the exit status

This script is simple but we still have to know how to make use of the exit codes from scripts and other applications. The command-line list that we generated earlier while creating the $HOME/bin directory, is a good example of how we can use the exit code:

```
$ command1 || command 2
```

In the preceding example, command2 is executed only if command1 fails in some way. To be specific, command2 will run if command1 exits with a status code other than 0.

Similarly, in the following extract:

```
$ command1 && command2
```

We will only execute command2 if command1 succeeds and issues an exit code of 0.

To read the exit code from our script explicitly, we can view the $?variable, as shown in the following example:

```
$ hello1.sh
```

```
$ echo $?
```

The expected output is 0, as this is what we have added to the last line of the file and there is precious little else that can go wrong causing us to fail in reaching that line.

Ensuring a unique name

We can now create and execute a simple script but we need to consider the name a little. In this case, `hello1.sh` is going to be good enough and is unlikely to clash with anything else on the system. We should avoid using names that may clash with existing aliases, functions, keywords, and building commands, as well as, avoid names of programs already in use.

Adding the `sh` suffix to the file does not guarantee the name to be unique but in Linux, where we do not file extensions, the suffix is a part of the file name. This helps you to provide a unique identity to your script. Additionally, the suffix is used by the editor to help you identify the file for syntax highlighting. If you recall, we specifically added the syntax highlighting file `sh.nanorc` to the nano text editor. Each of these files is specific to a suffix and subsequent language.

Referring back to the command hierarchy within this chapter, we can use a type to determine the location and type of file `hello.sh` is:

```
$ type hello1.sh   #To determine the type and path

$ type -a hello1.sh   #To print all commands found if the name is NOT
unique

$ type -t hello1.sh ~To print the simple type of the command
```

These commands and output can be seen in the following screenshot:

```
pi@pilabs ~ $ type hello1.sh
hello1.sh is hashed (/home/pi/bin/hello1.sh)
pi@pilabs ~ $ type -a hello1.sh
hello1.sh is /home/pi/bin/hello1.sh
pi@pilabs ~ $ type -t hello1.sh
file
pi@pilabs ~ $
```

Hello Dolly!

It is possible that we might need a little more substance in the script than a simple fixed message. Static message content does have its place but we can make this script much more useful by building some flexibility.

In this chapter, we will look at positional parameters or arguments that we can supply to the script and in the next chapter we will see how we can make the script interactive and also prompt the user for input at runtime.

Running the script with arguments

We can run the script with arguments, after all it's a free world and Linux promotes your freedom to do what you want to do with the code. However, if the script does not make use of the arguments, then they will be silently ignored. The following code shows the script running with a single argument:

```
$ hello1.shfred
```

The script will still run and will not produce an error. The output will not change either and will print hello world:

Argument Identifier	Description
$0	The name of the script itself and is often used in usage statements.
$1	Positional argument, the first argument passed to the script.
${10}	Where two or more digits are needed to represent the argument position. Brace brackets are used to delimit the variable name from any other content. Single value digits are expected.
$#	Argument count is especially useful when we need to set the amount of arguments needed for correct script execution.
$*	Refers to all arguments.

For the script to make use of the argument, we can change the script content a little. Let's first copy the script, add in the execute permissions, and then edit the new hello2.sh:

```
$ cp $HOME/bin/hello1.sh $HOME/bin/hello2.sh
```

```
$ chmod +x $HOME/bin/hello2.sh
```

We need to edit the hello2.sh file to make use of the argument as it is passed at the command line. The following screenshot shows the simplest use of command line arguments allowing us now to have a custom message.

```
#!/bin/bash
echo "Hello $1"
exit 0
~
```

Run the script now, we can provide an argument as shown in the following:

```
$ hello2.sh fred
```

The output should now say **Hello fred**. If we do not provide an argument then the variable will be empty and will just print **Hello**. You can refer to the following screenshot to see the execution argument and output:

```
pi@pilabs ~ $ hello2.sh fred
Hello fred
pi@pilabs ~ $ _
```

If we adjust the script to use $*, all the arguments will print. We will see **Hello** and then a list of all the supplied arguments. If we edit the script and replace the echo line as follows:

```
echo "Hello $*"
```

Executing the script with the following arguments:

```
$ hello2.shfredwilma  betty barney
```

Will result in the output shown in the following screenshot:

```
pi@pilabs ~ $
pi@pilabs ~ $ hello2.sh fred wilma betty barney
Hello fred wilma betty barney
pi@pilabs ~ $ _
```

If we want to print Hello <name>, each on separate lines, we will need to wait a little until we cover the looping structures. A for loop will work well to achieve this.

The importance of correct quotes

So far, we have used a simple double quoting mechanism to encase the strings that we want to use with echo.

In the first script, it does not matter if we use single or double quotes. The echo "Hello World" will be exactly the same as echo 'Hello World'.

However, this will not be the case in the second script so it is very important to understand the quoting mechanisms available in bash.

As we have seen, using the double quotes echo "Hello $1" will result in **Hello fred** or whatever the supplied value is. Whereas, if we use single quotes echo 'Hello $1' the printed output on the screen will be **Hello $1**, where we see the variable name and not its value.

The idea of the quotes is to protect the special character such as a space between the two words; both quotes protect the space from being interpreted. The space is normally read as a default field, separated by the shell. In other words, all characters are read by the shell as literals with no special meaning. This has the knock on effect of the $ symbol printing its literal format rather than allowing bash to expand its value. The bash shell is prevented from expanding the variable's value, as it is protected by the single quotes.

This is where the double quote comes to our rescue. The double quote will protect all the characters except the $, allowing bash to expand the stored value.

If we ever need to use a literal $ within the quoted string along with variables that need to be expanded; we can use double quotes but escape the desired $ with the backslash (\). For example, echo "$USER earns \$4" would print as **Fred earns $4** if the current user was Fred.

Try the following examples at the command line using all quoting mechanisms. Feel free to up your hourly rate as required:

```
$ echo "$USER earns $4"
$ echo '$USER earns $4'
$ echo "$USER earns \$4"
```

The output is shown in the following screenshot:

```
pi@pilabs ~ $ echo "$USER earns $4"
pi earns
pi@pilabs ~ $ echo '$USER earns $4'
$USER earns $4
pi@pilabs ~ $ echo "$USER earns \$4"
pi earns $4
pi@pilabs ~ $ _
```

Printing the script name

The $0 variable represents the script name and this is often used in usage statements. As we are not yet looking at conditional statements, we will have the script name printed above the displayed name.

Edit your script so that it reads as the following complete code block for $HOME/bin/ hello2.sh:

```
#!/bin/bash
echo "You are using $0"
echo "Hello $*"
exit 0
```

The output from the command is shown in the following screenshot:

```
pi@pilabs ~ $ hello2.sh fred
You are using /home/pi/bin/hello2.sh
Hello fred
pi@pilabs ~ $
```

If we prefer not to print the path and only want the name of the script to show we can use the basename command, which extracts the name from the path. Adjusting the script so that the second line now reads is as follows:

```
echo "You are using $(basename $0)"
```

The $(....) syntax is used to evaluate the output of the inner command. We first run basename $0 and feed the result into an unnamed variable represented by the $.

The new output will appear as seen in the following screenshot:

```
pi@pilabs ~ $ hello2.sh fred
You are using hello2.sh
Hello fred
```

It is possible to achieve the same results using back quotes, this is less easy to read but we have mentioned this as you might have to understand and modify the scripts that have been written by others. The alternative to the $(....) syntax is shown in the following example:

```
echo "You are using `basename $0`"
```

Please note that the characters used are back quotes and *NOT* single quotes. On UK and US keyboards, these are found in the top-left section next to the number *1* key.

Debugging your scripts

With the scripts as simple as we have seen so far, there is little that can go wrong or debug. As the script grows and decision paths are included with conditional statements, we may need to use some level of debugging to analyze the scripts progress better.

Bash provides two options for us, -v and -x.

If we want to look at the verbose output from our script and the detailed information about the way the script is evaluated line by line, we can use the -v option. This can be within the shebang but it is often easier to run the script directly with bash:

```
$ bash -v $HOME/bin/hello2.sh fred
```

This is especially useful in this example as we can see how each element of the embedded basename command is processed. The first step is removing the quotes and then the parentheses. Take a look at the following output:

```
pi@pilabs ~ $ bash -v $HOME/bin/hello2.sh fred
#!/bin/bash
echo "You are using $(basename $0)"
basename $0)"
basename $0)
basename $0
You are using hello2.sh
echo "Hello $*"
Hello fred
exit 0
pi@pilabs ~ $
```

More commonly used is the -x option, which displays the commands as they get executed. Its useful to know the decision branch that has been chosen by the script. The following shows this in use:

```
$ bash -x $HOME/bin/hello2.sh fred
```

We again see that the basename is evaluated first, but we do not see the more detailed steps involved in running that command. The screenshot that follows captures the command and output:

```
pi@pilabs ~ $ bash -x $HOME/bin/hello2.sh fred
++ basename /home/pi/bin/hello2.sh
+ echo 'You are using hello2.sh'
You are using hello2.sh
+ echo 'Hello fred'
Hello fred
+ exit 0
pi@pilabs ~ $
```

Summary

This marks the end of the chapter and I am sure that you might have found this useful. Especially for those making a start with bash scripting, this chapter must have built a firm foundation on which you can build your knowledge.

We began by ensuring that bash is secure and not susceptible to embedded functions shell-shock. With bash secured, we considered the execution hierarchy where aliases, functions, and so on are checked before the command; knowing this can help us plan a good naming structure and a path to locate the scripts.

Soon we were writing simple scripts with static content but we saw how easy it was to add flexibility using arguments. The exit code from the script can be read with the $? variable and we can create a command line list using || and &&, which depends on the success or failure of the preceding command in the list.

Finally, we closed the chapter by looking at debugging the script. Its not really required when the script is trivial, but it will be useful later when complexity is added.

In the next chapter, we will be creating interactive scripts that read the user's input during script execution.

Creating Interactive Scripts

2

In *Chapter 1, What and Why of Scripting with Bash*, of this book we learned how to create a script and use some of its basics elements. These include optional parameters that we can pass through to the script when it is executed. In this chapter, we will extend this by using the read shell built-in command to allow for interactive scripts. Interactive scripts are scripts that prompt for information during the script execution. In doing so, we will cover the following topics:

- Using `echo` with options
- Basic script using `read`
- Adding comments
- Enhancing `read` scripts with prompts
- Limiting the number of entered characters
- Control the visibility of the entered text
- Simple scripts to enforce our learning

Using echo with options

So far, in this book we have been able to see that the `echo` command is very useful and is going to be in many of our scripts, if not all. We have also seen that this is both a built-in command as well as a command file. When running the `echo` command, the built-in command will be used unless we state the full path to the file. We can test this with the following command:

```
$ test -a echo
```

To gain help on the built-in command, we can use `man bash` and search for echo; however, the `echo` command is identical to the internal command so I will recommend that you use `man echo` in most cases in order to display command options.

The basic use of echo that we have seen so far will produce a text output and a new line. This is often the desired response so we don't have to be concerned that the next prompt will append to the end of the echoed text. The new line separates the script output from the next shell prompt. If we do not supply any text string to print, echo will print only the new line to STDOUT. We can test this with the following command directly from the command line. We do not need to run echo or in fact any other command from a script. To run echo from the command line will simply enter the command as shown:

```
$ echo
```

The output will show a clear new line between the command we issued and the subsequent prompt. We can see this in the following screenshot:

```
pi@pilabs ~ $ echo

pi@pilabs ~ $ _
```

If we want to suppress the new line, especially useful if we are to prompt users, we can do this in the following two ways with the help of echo:

```
$ echo -n "Which directory do you want to use? "
$ echo -e "Which directory do you want to use? \c"
```

The result will be to suppress the line feed. In the initial example, the -n option is used to suppress the line feed. The second example uses the more generic -e option, which allows escape sequences to be added to the text string. To continue on the same line, we use \c as the escape sequence.

This does not look great as the final part of the script or when it is run from the command line, as the command prompt will follow. This is illustrated in the following screenshot:

```
pi@pilabs ~ $ echo -e "Which directory do you want to use? \c"
Which directory do you want to use? pi@pilabs ~ $ _
```

Basic script using read

When used as a part of a script that prompts for user input, the suppression of the line feed is exactly what we want. We will begin by copying the existing `hello2.sh` script to `hello3.sh` and build an interactive script. Initially, we will use `echo` as the prompt mechanism but as we gradually enhance the script, we will generate the prompt directly from the shell built-in `read` command:

```
$ cp $HOME/bin/hello2.sh $HOME/bin/hello3.sh
$ chmod +x $HOME/bin/hello3.sh
```

Edit the `$HOME/bin/hello3.sh` script so that it reads as the following:

```
#!/bin/bash
echo -n "Hello I  $(basename $0) may I ask your name: "
read
echo "Hello $REPLY"
exit 0
```

As we execute the script, we will be greeted and prompted with our own name. This is echoed out using the `$REPLY` variable in the `echo` statement. As we have not yet supplied a variable name to the `read` built-in command the default `$REPLY` variable is used. The script execution and output is shown in the following screenshot. Take some time to practice the script on your own system:

```
pi@pilabs ~ $ hello3.sh
Hello I  hello3.sh may I ask your name: fred
Hello fred
pi@pilabs ~ $ _
```

This little step has taken us a long way and there are many uses of a script like this, we have all used installation scripts that prompt for options and directories as we run through the install. I do accept that it is still quite trivial but as we delve into the chapter, we get closer to some more useful scripts.

Script comments

We should always introduce commenting scripts early in the piece. A script comment is prefaced with a # symbol. Anything after the # symbol is a comment and is not evaluated by the script. The shebang, `#!/bin/bash`, is primarily a comment and, as such, is not evaluated by the script. The shell running the script reads the shebang so it knows which command interpreter to hand the script over to. A comment may be at the start of a line or partly into the line. Shell scripting does not have the notion of multi-line comments.

If you are not already familiar with comments, then they are added to the script to tell all about who wrote the script, when it was written and last updated, and what the script does. It is the metadata of the script.

The following is an example of comments in scripts:

```
#!/bin/bash
# Welcome script to display a message to users on login
# Author: @theurbanpenguin
# Date: 1/1/1971
```

It is a good practice to comment and add comments that explain what the code is doing and why. This will help you and your colleagues, who need to edit the script at a later date.

Enhancing scripts with read prompts

We have seen how we can use the built in read to populate a variable. So far, we have used `echo` to produce the prompt but this can be passed to read itself using the `-p` option. The `read` command will surpass the additional linefeed, so we reduce both the line count and the complexity to some degree.

We can test this at the command line itself. Try typing the following command to see `read` in action:

$ read -p "Enter your name: " name

We use the `read` command with the `-p` option. The argument that follows the option is the text that appears in the prompt. Normally, we will make sure that there is a trailing space at the end of the text to ensure that we can clearly see what we type. The last argument supplied here is the variable we want to populate, we simply call it `name`. Variables are case-sensitive too. Even if we did not supply the last argument, we can still store the user's response, but this time in the `REPLY` variable.

 Note that when we return the value of a variable we use $ but not when we write it. In simple terms when reading a variable we refer to $VAR when setting a variable we refer to VAR=value.

The following illustration shows the `read` command with syntax using the `-p` option:

read -p <prompt> <variable name>

We can edit the script so that it appears similar to the following extract from `hello3.sh`:

```
#!/bin/bash
read -p "May I ask your name: " name
echo "Hello $name"
exit 0
```

The `read` prompt cannot evaluate commands within the message string, such as we used before.

Limiting the number of entered characters

We do not need functionality in the scripts we have used so far, but we may need to ask users to hit any key to continue. At the moment, we have set it up in such a way that the variable is not populated until we hit the *Enter* key. Users have to hit *Enter* to continue. If we use the `-n` option followed by an integer, we can specify the characters to accept before continuing, we will set 1 in this case. Take a look at the following code extract:

```
#!/bin/bash
read -p "May I ask your name: " name
echo "Hello $name"
read -n1 -p "Press any key to exit"
echo
exit 0
```

Now, the script will pause after displaying the name until we press any key; literally, we can press any key before continuing, as we accept just 1 key stroke. Whereas, earlier we were required to leave the default behavior in place, as we could not know how long a entered name would be. We have to wait for the user to hit *Enter*.

> Note that we add an additional echo here to ensure that a new line is issued before the script ends. This ensures that the shell prompt starts on a new line.

Controlling the visibility of entered text

Even though we have limited the input to a single character, we do get to see the text on the screen. In the same way, if we type the name we get to see the entered text before we hit *Enter*. In this case, it is just untidy but if we were entering sensitive data, such as a pin or a password, we should hide the text. We can use the silent option or -s to achieve this. A simple edit in the script will set this in place:

```
#!/bin/bash
read -p "May I ask your name: " name
echo "Hello $name"
read -sn1 -p "Press any key to exit"
echo
exit 0
```

Now, when we use a key to continue, it will not be displayed on the screen. We can see the behavior of the script in the following screenshot:

```
pi@pilabs ~ $ hello3.sh
May I ask your name: fred          We see the entered text
Hello fred
Press any key to continue    With -s we don't see the entered text
pi@pilabs ~ $ _
```

Enhancing learning with simple scripts

Our scripts are still a little trivial and we have not looked at conditional statements, so we can test for correct input, but let's take a look at some simple scripts that we can build with some functionality.

Backing-up with scripts

Now that we have created some scripts, we may want to back these up in a different location. If we create a script to prompt us, we can choose the location and the type of files that we want to backup.

Consider the following script for your first practice. Create the script and name it as $HOME/backup.sh:

```
#!/bin/bash
# Author: @theurbanpenguin
# Web: www.theurbapenguin.com
# Script to prompt to back up files and location
# The files will be search on from the user's home
```

```
# directory and can only be backed up to a directory
# within $HOME
# Last Edited: July 4 2015
read -p "Which file types do you want to backup " file_suffix
read -p "Which directory do you want to backup to " dir_name
# The next lines creates the directory if it does not exist
test -d $HOME/$dir_name || mkdir -m 700 $HOME/$dir_name
# The find command will copy files the match the
# search criteria ie .sh . The -path, -prune and -o
# options are to exclude the backdirectory from the
# backup.
find $HOME -path $HOME/$dir_name -prune -o \
 -name "*$file_suffix" -exec cp {} $HOME/$dir_name/ \;
exit 0
```

You will see that the file is commented; though as black and white the readability is a little difficult. If you have an electronic copy of the book, you should see the colors in the following screenshot:

```
#!/bin/bash
# Author: @theurbanpenguin
# Web: www.theurbapenguin.com
# Script to prompt to back up files and location
# The files will be search on from the user's home
# directory and can only be backed up to a directory
# within $HOME
# Last Edited: July 4 2015
read -p "Which file types do you want to backup " file_suffix
read -p "Which directory do you want to backup to " dir_name
# The next lines creates the directory if it does not exist
test -d $HOME/$dir_name || mkdir -m 700 $HOME/$dir_name
# The find command will copy files the match the
# search criteria ie .sh . The -path, -prune and -o
# options are to exclude the backdirectory from the
# backup.
find $HOME -path $HOME/$dir_name -prune -o \
 -name "*$file_suffix" -exec cp {} $HOME/$dir_name/ \;
exit 0
```

As the script runs, you may choose .sh for the files to backup and backup as the directory. The script execution is shown in the following screenshot along with a listing of the directory:

```
pi@pilabs ~ $ backup.sh
Which file types do you want to backup .sh
Which directory do you want to backup to backup
pi@pilabs ~ $ ls $HOME/backup
autogunk.sh          ECCcertgen.sh      irix.sh
autoungunk.sh        ECC-RSAcertgen.sh  launcher.sh
backup.sh            fixNT.sh           mkcerts.sh
bat.sh               FreeBSD.sh         mksmime-certs.sh
c89.sh               hello1.sh          opensslwrap.sh
CA.sh                hello2.sh          point.sh
connect_server.sh    hello3.sh          profile.sh
cygwin.sh            hpux10-cc.sh       pthread2.sh
do_ms.sh             install.sh         pthread.sh
pi@pilabs ~ $ _
```

Now you can see if we can start to create meaningful scripts with trivial scripting; although I will strongly urge adding error checking the user input if this script has to be for something other than personal use. As we progress into the book will cover this.

Connecting to a server

Let's look at some practical scripts that we can use to connect to servers. First, we will look at ping and in the second script we will look at prompting for SSH credentials.

Version 1 – ping

This is something we all can do as no special services are required. This will simplify the ping command for console users who may not know the details of the command. This will ping the server for just three counts rather than the normal infinite amount. There is no output if the server is alive but a failed server reports Sever dead. Create the script as $HOME/bin/ping_server.sh:

```
#!/bin/bash
# Author: @theurbanpenguin
# Web: www.theurbapenguin.com
# Script to ping a server
# Last Edited: July 4 2015
read -p "Which server should be pinged " server_addr
ping -c3 $server_addr 2>&1 > /dev/null || echo "Server dead"
```

The following screenshot shows successful and failed output:

```
pi@pilabs ~ $
pi@pilabs ~ $ ping_server.sh
Which server should be pinged localhost
pi@pilabs ~ $ ping_server.sh
Which server should be pinged 1.2.3.4
Server Dead
pi@pilabs ~ $ _
```

Version 2 – SSH

Often SSH is installed and running on servers, so you may be able to run this script if your system is running SSH or you have access to an SSH server. In this script, we prompt for the server address and username and pass them through to the SSH client. Create the script as `$HOME/bin/connect_server.sh`:

```
#!/bin/bash
# Author: @theurbanpenguin
# Web: www.theurbapenguin.com
# Script to prompt fossh connection
# Last Edited: July 4 2015
read -p "Which server do you want to connect to: " server_name
read -p "Which username do you want to use: " user_name
ssh ${user_name}@$server_name
```

 Note the use of the brace bracket to delimit the variable from the @ symbol in the last line of the script.

Version 3 – MySQL/MariaDB

In the next script, we will provide the detail for a database connection along with the SQL query to execute. You will be able to run this if you have a MariaDB or MySQL database server on your system or one that you can connect to. For the demonstration, I will use a Raspberry Pi running Ubuntu-Mate 15.04 and MariaDB version 10; however, this should work for any MySQL server or MariaDB from version 5 onwards. The script collects user and password information as well as the SQL command to execute. Create the script as `$HOME/bin/run_mql.sh`:

```
#!/bin/bash
# Author: @theurbanpenguin
# Web: www.theurbapenguin.com
```

```
# Script to prompt for MYSQL user password and command
# Last Edited: July 4 2015
read -p "MySQL User: " user_name
read -sp "MySQL Password: " mysql_pwd
echo
read -p "MySQL Command: " mysql_cmd
read -p "MySQL Database: " mysql_db
mysql -u $user_name -p$mysql_pwd$mysql_db -e"$mysql_cmd"
```

In the script, we can see that we suppress the display of the MySQL password when we input it into the read command using the -s option. Again, we use echo directly to ensure that the next prompt starts on a new line.

The script input is shown in the following screenshot:

```
andrew@web:~$ ./run_mysql.sh
MySQL User: andrew
MySQL Password:
MySQL Command: SHOW TABLES;
MySQL DB: wordpress
Tables_in_wordpress
wp_cleanup_optimizer_block_range_ip
wp_cleanup_optimizer_block_single_ip
wp_cleanup_optimizer_db_scheduler
wp_cleanup_optimizer_licensing
wp_cleanup_optimizer_login_log
wp_cleanup_optimizer_plugin_settings
wp_cleanup_optimizer_wp_scheduler
```

Now, we can easily see the password suppression working and the ease of adding to the MySQL commands.

Summary

Feel proud that you have your "I can read" badge for shell scripting. We have developed our scripts to be interactive and prompting users for input during the script execution. These prompts can be used to simplify user operations on the command line. In this way, they do not need to remember the command line options or have passwords that end up stored in the command line history. When using passwords, we can silently store the value using the read -sp options.

In the next chapter, we will take our time to look at the conditional statements in bash.

3

Conditions Attached

I suppose we can say that we are now into the fine print of the script. These are the details that are written into our scripts using conditions to test if a statement should run or not. We are now ready to add some intelligence in scripts so our scripts become more robust, easier to use, and more reliable. Conditional statements can be written with simple command-line lists of AND or OR commands together or, more often, within traditional if statements.

In this chapter we will cover the following topics:

- Simple decision paths using command-line lists
- Verifying user input with lists
- Using the test shell built-in
- Creating conditional statements using if
- Extending if with else
- More conditions with elif
- Creating the backup.sh script using elif
- Using case statements
- Script – front-end with grep

Simple decision paths using command-line lists

We have used command-line lists both in *Chapter 1, What and Why of Scripting with Bash* of this book and in some of the scripts found in *Chapter 2, Creating Interactive Scripts*. Lists are one of the simplest conditional statements that we can create and so we thought that it was appropriate to use them in the earlier examples before fully explaining them here.

Command-line lists are two or more statements that are joined using either the AND or OR notations:

- && : AND
- || : OR

Where the two statements are joined using the AND notation, the second command only runs if the first command succeeds. Whereas, with the OR notation the second command will run only if the first command fails.

The decision of the success or failure of a command is taken by reading the exit code from the application. A zero represents a successful application completion and anything other than a zero will represent a failure. We can test the success or failure of an application by reading the exit status by means of the system variables $?. This is shown in the following example:

```
$ echo $?
```

If we need to ensure that a script is run from a user's home directory, we can build this into the script's logic. This can be tested from the command line and it does not have to be in a script. Consider the following command-line example:

```
$ test $PWD == $HOME || cd $HOME
```

The double vertical bars denote an OR list. This ensures that the second statement is only executed when the first statement is not true. In simple terms, if we are not currently in the home directory we will be by the end of the command-line list. We will see more on the test command soon.

We can build this into almost any command that we want and not just test. For example, we can query to see if a user is logged into the system, if they are then we can use the write command to directly message their console. Similar as before, we can test this in the command line prior to adding it to the script. This is shown in the following command-line example:

```
$ who | grep pi > /dev/null 2>&1 && write pi < message.txt
```

If we use this in a script, it is almost certain that we will replace the username with a variable. In general, if we have to refer to the same value more than once then a variable is a good idea. In this case, we are searching for the pi user.

When we break the command-line list down, we first use the who command to list the users who are logged on. We pipe the list to grep to search for the desired username. We are not interested in the output from the search, just the success or failure. With this in mind, we redirect all our output to /dev/null. The double ampersand indicates that the second statement in the list runs only if the first returns true. If the pi user is logged on, we use write to message the user. The following screenshot illustrates this command and the output.

```
pi@pilabs: ~
pi@pilabs ~ $ who | grep pi > /dev/null 2>&1 && write pi < message.txt

Message from pi@pilabs.theurbanpenguin.com on pts/0 at 10:42 ...
I see you are logged on then!

EOF
pi@pilabs ~ $ _
```

Verifying user input with lists

In this script, we will ensure that a value has been supplied to the first positional parameter. We can modify the hello2.sh script that we created in *Chapter 1, What and Why of Scripting with Bash*, to check for user input before displaying the hello text.

You can copy the hello2.sh script to hello4.sh or simply create a new script from scratch. There will not be a lot a typing and the script will be created as $HOME/bin/hello4.sh, as shown:

```
#!/bin/bash
echo "You are using $(basename $0)"
test -z $1 || echo "Hello $1"
exit 0
~
```

We can ensure that the script is executable with the following command:

```
$ chmod +x $HOME/bin/hello4.sh
```

We can then run the script with or without arguments. The test statement is looking for the $1 variable to be zero bytes. If it is, then we will not see the hello statement; otherwise it will print the **Hello** message. In simple terms, we will see the hello message if we supply a name.

The following screenshot shows the output that you will see when you do not supply a parameter to the script, followed by the supplied parameter:

```
pi@pilabs: ~/bin
pi@pilabs ~/bin $ hello4.sh
You are using hello4.sh
pi@pilabs ~/bin $ hello4.sh bob
You are using hello4.sh
Hello bob
pi@pilabs ~/bin $ _
```

Using the test shell builtin

It is probably time for us to pull over to the side of the scripting highway and look a little more at this command test. This is both a shell builtin and a file executable in its own right. Of course, we will have to hit the built-in command first, unless we specify the full path to the file.

When the test command is run without any expressions to evaluate, then the test will return false. So, if we run the test as shown in the following command:

```
$ test
```

The exit status will be 1, even though no error output is shown. The test command will always return either True or False or 0 or 1, respectively. The basic syntax of test is:

```
test EXPRESSION
```

Or, we can inverse the test command with:

```
test ! EXPRESSION
```

If we need to include multiple expressions, these can be AND or OR together using the -a and -o options, respectively:

```
test EXPRESSION -a EXPRESSION
```
```
test EXPRESSION -o EXPRESSION
```

We can also write in a shorthand version replacing the test with square brackets to surround the expression as shown in the following example:

```
[ EXPRESION ]
```

Testing strings

We can test for the equality or inequality of two strings. For example, one of the ways to test the root user is using the following command:

```
test $USER = root
```

We could also write this using the square bracket notation:

```
[ $USER = root ]
```

Equally, we could test for a non-root account with the following two methods:

```
test ! $USER = root
[ ! $USER = root ]
```

We can also test for zero values and non-zero values of strings. We saw this in an earlier example in this chapter.

To test if a string has a value, we could use the -n option. We can check to see if the current connection is made via SSH by checking for the existence of a variable in the user's environment. We show this using test and square brackets in the following two examples:

```
test -n $SSH_TTY
[ -n $SSH_TTY ]
```

If this is true, then the connection is made with SSH; if it is false, then the connection is not via SSH.

As we saw earlier, testing for a zero string value is useful when deciding if a variable is set:

```
test -z $1
```

Or, more simply, we could use:

```
[ -z $1 ]
```

A true result for this query means that no input parameters have been supplied to the script.

Testing integers

As well as, testing string values of bash scripts can test for integer values and whole numbers. Another way of testing input of a script is to count the numbers of positional parameters and also test that the number is above 0:

```
test $# -gt 0
```

Or using the brackets, as shown:

```
[ $# -gt 0 ]
```

When in relationship, top positional parameters the variable $# represents the number of parameters passed to the script. To test equality of integer values, the -eq option is used and not the = symbol.

Testing file types

While testing for values we can test for the existence of a file or file type. For example, we may only want to delete a file if it is a symbolic link. I use this while compiling a kernel. The /usr/src/linux directory should be a symbolic link to the latest kernel source code. If I download a newer version before compiling the new kernel, I need to delete the existing link and create a new link. Just in case someone has created the /usr/src/linux directory, we can test it as a link before removing it:

```
# [ -h /usr/src/linux ] &&rm /usr/src/linux
```

The -h option tests that the file has a link. Other options include:

- -d: This shows that it's a directory
- -e: This shows that the file exists in any form
- -x: This shows that the file is executable
- -f: This shows that the file is a regular file
- -r: This shows that the file is readable
- -p: This shows that the file is a named pipe
- -b: This shows that the file is a block device
- -c: This shows that the file is a character device

More options do exist, so delve into the main pages as you need. We will use different options throughout the book; thus, giving you practical and useful examples.

Creating conditional statements using if

As we have seen so far, it is possible to build simple conditions using command-line lists. These conditionals can be written both with and without a test. As the complexity of the tasks increases, it will be easier to create statements using if. This certainly will ease both the readability of the script and the logic layout. To a degree, it also matches the way in which we think and speak, if is a semantic in our spoken language as it is within the bash script.

Even though it will take up more than a single line in the script, with an `if` statement we can achieve more and make the script more legible. With that said, let's look at creating `if` conditions. The following is an example of a script using an `if` statement:

```
#!/bin/bash
# Welcome script to display a message to users
# Author: @theurbanpenguin
# Date: 1/1/1971
if [ $# -lt 1 ] ; then
echo "Usage: $0 <name>"
exit 1
fi
echo "Hello $1"
exit 0
```

The code within the `if` statement will run only when the condition evaluates to true and the end of the `if` block is denoted with `fi` - if backwards. The color coding in `vim` can be useful to aide readability, which you may see in the following screenshot:

```
#!/bin/bash
# Welcome script to display a message to users on login
# Author: @theurbanpenguin
# Date: 1/1/1971
if [ $# -lt 1 ] ; then
    echo "Usage: $0 <name>"
    exit 1
fi
echo "Hello $1"
exit 0
```

Within the script, we can easily add in multiple statements to run when the condition is true. In our case, this includes exiting the script with an error indicated, as well as, the `usage` statement to assist the user. This ensures that we only display the **Hello** message if we have supplied a name to be welcomed.

We can view the script execution both with and without the argument in the following screenshot:

```
pi@pilabs ~ $ hello5.sh
Usage: /home/pi/bin/hello5.sh <name>
pi@pilabs ~ $ hello5.sh  fred
Hello fred
pi@pilabs ~ $ _
```

To help us understand the layout of the `if` conditional statement, the following illustration demonstrates the syntax using a pseudo-code:

```
if condition ; then
        statement 1
        statement 2
fi
```

Indenting the code is not required but it helps readability and is highly recommended. Adding the `then` statement to the same line as the `if`, again, assists in the readability of the code and the semi-colon is required to separate the `if` from the `then`.

Extending if with else

When a script is required to continue regardless of the result of the `if` condition, it is often necessary to deal with both conditions of the evaluation. What to do when it is true, as well as, false. This is where we can make use of the `else` keyword. This allows the execution of one block of code when the condition is true and another when the condition is evaluated as false. The pseudo-code for this is shown in the next illustration:

```
if condition ; then
        statement
else
        statement
fi
```

If we consider extending the `hello5.sh` script that we created earlier, it is easily possible to allow for correct execution regardless of the parameter being present or not. We can recreate this as `hello6.sh`, as follows:

```
#!/bin/bash
# Welcome script to display a message to users
# Author: @theurbanpenguin
# Date: 1/1/1971
if [ $# -lt 1 ] ; then
read -p "Enter a name: "
name=$REPLY
```

```
else
name=$1
fi
echo "Hello $name"
exit 0
```

The script sets a named variable now, it helps readability and we can assign the correct value to $name from the input parameter or from the read prompt, either way the script is working well and starting to take shape.

More conditions with elif

Moving onto where we require a greater degree of control, we can use the elif keyword. Unlike else, elif requires an additional condition to be tested for each elif. In this way, we can provide for different circumstances. We can add in as many elif conditions as required. The following shows a pseudo-code:

```
if condition; then
statement
elif condition; then
statement
else
statement
fi
exit 0
```

A script may make life easier for the operator by providing a simplified selection for a more complex code. Even though the script becomes gradually more complex to meet the requirements, to the operator the execution is greatly simplified. It is our job to enable users to run more complex operations easily from the command line when creating scripts. Often, this will necessitate the addition of more complexity to our scripts; however, we will be rewarded with the reliability of the scripted application.

Creating the backup2.sh using elif

We can revisit the script that we created to run the earlier backup. This script, $HOME/bin/backup.sh, prompts the user for the file type and the directory to store the backup. The tools used for the backup are find and cp.

With this new found knowledge, we can now allow the script to run the backup using the command tar and the level of compression selected by the operator. There is no requirement, to select the file type as the complete home directory will be backed up with the exclusion of the backup directory itself.

The operator can select the compression based on three letters H, M, and L. The selection will affect the options passed to the `tar` command and the backup file created. The selection of high will be using `bzip2` compression, medium using `gzip` compression and low creating an uncompressed `tar` archive. The logic exists in the extended `if` statement that follows:

```
if [ $file_compression = "L" ] ; then
tar_opt=$tar_l
elif [ $file_compression = "M" ]; then
tar_opt=$tar_m
else
tar_opt=$tar_h
fi
```

Based on the user selection, we can configure the correct options for the `tar` command. As we have three conditions to evaluate the `if`, `elif`, and `else` statements are appropriate. To see how the variables are configured we can view the following extract from the script:

```
tar_l="-cvf $backup_dir/b.tar --exclude $backup_dir $HOME"
tar_m="-czvf $backup_dir/b.tar.gz --exclude $backup_dir $HOME"
tar_h="-cjvf $backup_dir/b.tar.bzip2 --exclude $backup_dir $HOME"
```

The complete script can be created as `$HOME/bin/backup2.sh` and should read as the following code:

```
#!/bin/bash
# Author: @theurbanpenguin
# Web: www.theurbapenguin.com
read -p "Choose H, M or L compression " file_compression
read -p "Which directory do you want to backup to " dir_name
# The next lines creates the directory if it does not exist
test -d $HOME/$dir_name || mkdir -m 700 $HOME/$dir_name
backup_dir=$HOME/$dir_name
tar_l="-cvf $backup_dir/b.tar --exclude $backup_dir $HOME"
tar_m="-czvf $backup_dir/b.tar.gz --exclude $backup_dir $HOME"
tar_h="-cjvf $backup_dir/b.tar.bzip2 --exclude $backup_dir $HOME"
if [ $file_compression = "L" ] ; then
tar_opt=$tar_l
elif [ $file_compression = "M" ]; then
tar_opt=$tar_m
else
tar_opt=$tar_h
fi
tar $tar_opt
exit 0
```

When we execute the script we need to select H, M, or L in upper-case as this is how the selection is made within the script. The following screenshot shows the initial script execution where the selection for M has been made:

```
pi@pilabs ~ $ backup2.sh
Choose H, M or L compression M_
```

Using case statements

Rather than using multiple elif statements, a case statement may provide a simpler mechanism when evaluations are made on a single expression.

The basic layout of a case statement is listed below using pseudo-code:

```
case expression in
 case1)
   statement1
   statement2
 ;;
 case2)
   statement1
   statement2
 ;;
 *)
   statement1
 ;;
esac
```

The statement layout that we see is not dissimilar to switch statements that exist in other languages. In bash, we can use the case statement to test for simple values, such as strings or integers. Case statements can cater for a side range of letters, such as [a-f] or a through to f, but they cannot easily deal with integer ranges such as [1-20].

The case statement will first expand the expression and then it will try to match it in turn with each item. When a match is found, all the statements are executed until the ;;. This indicates the end of the code for that match. If there is no match, the case else statement indicated by the * will be matched. This needs to be the last item in the list.

Consider the following script `grade.sh`, used to evaluate grades:

```
#!/bin/bash
# Script to evaluate grades
# Usage: grade.sh student grade
# Author: @theurbanpenguin
# Date: 1/1/1971
if [ ! $# -eq2 ] ; then
echo "You must provide <student><grade>
exit 2
fi
case $2 in
   [A-C]|[a-c]) echo "$1 is a star pupil"
   ;;
   [Dd]) echo "$1 needs to try a little harder!"
   ;;
   [E-F]|[e-f]) echo "$1 could do a lot better next year"
   ;;
   *) echo "Grade could not be evaluated for $1"
esac
```

The script first uses an `if` statement to check that exactly two arguments have been supplied to the script. If they are not supplied, the script will exit with an error state:

```
if [ ! $# -eq2 ] ; then
echo "You must provide <student><grade>
exit 2
fi
```

The `case` statement then expands the expression, which is the value of the $2 variable in this example. This represents the grade that we supply. We then try to match first against the letters A through to C in both upper-case and lower-case. [A-C] is used to match A or B or C. The vertical bar then adds an additional OR to compare with a, b, or c:

```
[A-C]|[a-c]) echo "$1 is a star pupil"
;;
```

We make similar tests for other supplied grades A through to F.

The following screenshot show the script execution with different grades:

```
pi@pilabs ~/bin $ grade.sh Bob b
Bob is a star pupil
pi@pilabs ~/bin $ grade.sh Bob D
Bob needs to try a little harder!
pi@pilabs ~/bin $ grade.sh Bob e
Bob could do a lot better next year
pi@pilabs ~/bin $ grade.sh Bob 5
Grade could not be evaluated for Bob 5
pi@pilabs ~/bin $ _
```

Script – building a front-end with grep

As a finale to this chapter, we can group a few features that we have learned together and build a script that prompts the operator for a filename, a search string, and an operation to carry out with the grep command. We can create the script as $HOME/bin/search.sh and don't forget to make it executable:

```
#!/bin/bash
#Author: @theurbanpenguin
usage="Usage: search.sh file string operation"

if [ ! $# -eq3 ] ; then
echo "$usage"
exit 2
fi

[ ! -f $1 ]&& exit 3

case $3 in
    [cC])
mesg="Counting the matches in $1 of $2"
opt="-c"
```

```
    ;;
    [pP])
mesg="Print the matches of $2 in $1"
        opt=""
    ;;
    [dD])
mesg="Printing all lines but those matching $3 from $1"
opt="-v"
    ;;
    *) echo "Could not evaluate $1 $2 $3";;
esac
echo $mesg
grep $opt $2 $1
```

We start by checking for exactly three input arguments using the following code:

```
if [ ! $# -eq3 ] ; then
echo "$usage"
exit 2
fi
```

The next check uses a command-line list to exit the script if the file argument is not a regular file using `test -f`:

```
[ ! -f $1 ]&& exit 3
```

The `case` statement allows for three operations:

- Counting the matching lines
- Printing the matching lines
- Printing all but the matching lines

The following screenshot shows the search of `/etc/ntp.conf` file for lines beginning with the string server. We choose the count option in this example:

```
pi@pilabs ~ $ search.sh /etc/ntp.conf ^server c
Counting the matches in /etc/ntp.conf of ^server
4
pi@pilabs ~ $ _
```

Summary

One of the most important and time consuming tasks in scripting is building all of the conditional statements that we need to make the script usable and robust. There is an 80-20 rule that is often spoken of. This is where 20 percent of your time is spent in writing the main script and 80 percent of the time is spent to ensure all of the possible eventualities that are correctly handled in the script. This is what I refer to as the procedural integrity of the script, where we try to cover each scenario carefully and accurately.

We started by looking at a simple test with command-line lists. If the actions needed are simple, then these provide great functionality and are easily added. Where more complexity is required, we will add `if` statements.

Using the `if` statements, we can extend them as required using the `else` and `elif` keywords. Don't forget that `elif` keywords need their own conditions to evaluate.

Finally, we saw how we can use `case` where a single expression needs to be evaluated.

In the next chapter, we will understand the importance of reading in from already prepared code snippets. We will create a sample `if` statement that can be saved as code snippets to be read into the script at the time of editing.

4
Creating Code Snippets

If you like using the command line, but also like some of the features associated with using graphical **Integrated Development Environments (IDEs)**, then this chapter may reveal some new ideas to you. We can create shortcuts for commonly used script elements using the vi or vim text editors from the command line.

In this chapter, we will cover the following topics:

- Creating abbreviations in .vimrc
- Reading snippets with vim text editor
- Using color in terminal

Abbreviations

We have already taken one short sojourn into the ~/.vimrc file and we will now revisit this file to look at abbreviations or abbr controls. This file acts as the run control mechanism for the vim text editor, which is likely to be installed on your Linux distribution. Older distributions or Unix variants may have the original vi text editor and will make use of the ~/.exrc file. If you are uncertain of the identity of your version of vi and the correct run control file to use, simply, enter the vi command. If a blank page opens, it is indeed vi. However, if a new blank document opens with the vim splash screens, then you are using the improved vim or Vi.

Abbreviations allow for a shortcut string to be used in place of a longer string. These abbreviations can be set during a vim session from the last line mode but are often set in the control file. The shebang can be easily represented by an abbreviation, as follows:

```
abbr _sh #!/bin/bash
```

The basic syntax of an abbreviation is shown in the following command:

```
abbr <shortcut><string>
```

Using this abbreviation, we just need to type _sh while in the edit mode. On pressing the *ENTER* key after the shortcut code, the full text for the shebang is printed. In reality, not just the *ENTER* key but pressing any key after the `abbr` code will expand the shortcut. Simple elements like this can add a lot to the experience of using `vim` as our text editor. The following screenshot shows the updated `~/.vimrc` file:

We are not limited to the single abbreviation code, as we can add more `abbr` entries. For example, to support the shebang for Perl scripts at the line:

```
abbr _pl #!/usr/bin/perl
```

The use of the underscore is not required, but the aim is to keep the shortcut code unique and not to have a typed error. We are also not limited to a single line; although, this is where abbreviations are most used. Consider the following abbreviation for an `if` statement:

```
abbr _if if [-z $1];then<CR>echo "> $0 <name><CR>exit 2<CR>fi
```

Although this does work, the formatting of the `if` statement will not be perfect and multiline abbreviations are far from ideal. This is where we may consider using code snippets that we prepared in advance.

Using code snippets

All we mean by the term code snippets is a prepared code that we can read into our current script. This is especially easy with `vim` being able to read the contents of other text files during editing:

```
ESC
:r <path-and-filename>
```

For example, if we need to read the contents of a file called `if` located in `$HOME/snippets`, we will use the following key sequences in `vim`:

```
ESC
:r $HOME/snippets/if
```

The contents of this file is read into the current document below the current cursor position. In this way, we can make the code snippets as complex as we need and maintain the correct indentations to aide readability and consistency.

So, we will make it our duty to always create a snippets directory in our home directory:

```
$ mkdir -m 700 $HOME/snippets
```

It is not required to share the directory, so it is good practice to set the mode to `700` or private to the user when it is being created.

When creating snippets, it is your choice to use a pseudo-code or real examples. My preference is to use real examples that are edited to reflect the requirements of the recipient script. The contents of a simple `if` snippet will be:

```
if [ -z $1 ] ; then
    echo "Usage: $0 <name>"
    exit 2
fi
```

This gives us the layout to create an `if` statement with a practical example. In this case, we check to see if `$1` is unset and send an error to the user before exiting the script. The key is in keeping the snippet short to limit the changes that need to be made but easily understood and expandable, as required.

Bringing color to the terminal

If we are to display text messages to the users and operators executing the scripts, we can provide colors to help in message interpretation. Using red as a synonym for errors and green indicating success makes it easier to add functionality to our scripts. Not all but certainly a vast majority of Linux terminals support color. The built-in command `echo` when used with the `-e` option can display color to users.

To display a text in red we can use the `echo` command, as follows:

```
$ echo -e "\033[31mError\033[0m"
```

The following screenshot shows both the code and the output:

```
pi@pilabs ~ $ echo -e "\033[31mError\033[0m"
Error
```

The red text will bring immediate attention to the text and the potential of failure of script execution. The use of color in this way adheres to the basics of principals application design. If you find the code cumbersome, then simply use friendly variables to represent the colors and the reset code.

In the previous code, we used red and the final rest code to set the text back to the shell default. We could easily create variables for these color codes and others:

```
RED="\033[31m"
GREEN="\033[32m"
BLUE="\033[34m"
RESET="\033[0m"
```

The \033 value is the *ESCAPE* character and [31m is the color code for red.

We need to take care while using variables, to ensure that they are properly delimited from the text. Modifying the earlier example, we can see how this is easily achieved:

```
$ echo -e ${RED}Error$RESET"
```

We use the brace brackets to ensure that the RED variable is identified and separated from the Error word.

Saving the variable definitions to the $HOME/snippets/color file will allow them to be used in other scripts. Interestingly, we don't need to edit this script; we can use the command source to read these variables definitions into the script at runtime. Within the recipient script, we need to add the following line:

```
source $HOME/snippets/color
```

Using the shell built-in source command will read the color variables into the script executing at runtime. The following screenshot shows a modified version of the hello5.sh script that we now call hello7.sh, which makes use of these colors:

```
pi@pilabs: ~/bin
#!/bin/bash
# Welcome script to display a message to users on login
# Author: @theurbanpenguin
# Date: 1/1/1971
source $HOME/snippets/color
if [ $# -lt 1 ] ; then
  echo -e "${RED}Usage: $0 <name>$RESET"
  exit 1
fi
echo -e "${GREEN}Hello $1$RESET"
exit 0
```

We can see the effect this has when we execute the script. In the following screenshot, you will see the execution and output both with and without a supplied parameter:

```
pi@pilabs ~/bin $ hello7.sh fred
Hello fred
pi@pilabs ~/bin $ hello7.sh
Usage: /home/pi/bin/hello7.sh <name>
pi@pilabs ~/bin $ _
```

We can easily identify the success and failure of the script via the color coded output; the green **Hello fred** where we supply the parameter and the red Usage statement where we have not provided the required name.

Summary

To any administrator script reuse will always be upmost in the quest for efficiency. Using vim at the command line can make for very quick and effective editing of a script and we can save typing in the use of abbreviations. These are best set within a user's personal .vimrc file and are defined with the abbr control. Beyond abbreviations, we can see the sense in using code snippets. These are pre-prepared blocks of code that can be read into the current script.

Finally, we had a look at the value in using color at the command line where a script will provide feedback. In the first look, these color codes are not the friendliest, but we can simplify the process by using variables. These variables can be set at runtime within the script and by using the source command their values to read them into the current environment.

In the next chapter, we will look at other mechanisms that we can use to write test expressions simplifying the use of integers and variables.

5
Alternative Syntax

So far in the scripting journey, we have seen that we can use the `test` command to determine a conditional status. We have taken this a little further and discovered that we can also make use of the single square bracket. Here, we will recap the `test` command and look at the single square bracket in more detail. After having learned more about the square bracket, we will move onto more advanced variable or parameter management; thus, providing defaults and understating quoting issues.

Finally, we are going to see that within advanced shells like bash, korn, and zsh we can go with double brackets! Making use of the double round parenthesis and double square bracket can simplify the overall syntax and allow the standardization of the use of mathematical symbols.

In this chapter, we will cover the following topics:

- Test conditions
- Providing parameter defaults
- When in doubt – quote!
- Advanced tests using `[[`
- Advanced tests using `((`

Recapping test

So far we have used the built-in `test` command to drive our conditional statements. Using other options with `test`, we can look at the returned value to determine the status of files in the file system. Running the test without any option will return a false output:

```
$ test
```

Testing files

Commonly, we can use `test` to check the conditions based around files.
For example, to test that a file is present, or not, we can use the `-e` option.
The following command will test the existence of the `/etc/hosts` file:

```
test -e /etc/hosts
```

We can run this test again, but this time check that the file not only exists but is a regular file as opposed to having some special purpose. Specific file types can be directories, pipes, links, and so on. The option for a regular file is `-f`.

```
$ test -f /etc/hosts
```

Adding logic

If we need to open a file from within our script, we will test that the file is both a regular file and has the read permission set. To achieve this with `test`, we can also include the `-a` option to AND multiple conditions together. In the following example code, we will use the `-r` condition to check that the file is readable:

```
$ test -f /etc/hosts -a -r /etc/hosts
```

Similarly, the use of `-o` is supported to OR two conditions within an expression.

Square brackets as not seen before

As an alternative to the `test` command, we can implement the same conditional tests using the single square bracket. Repeating the previous conditional test and omitting the command itself. We will rewrite this, as shown in the following code:

```
$ [ -f /etc/hosts -a -r /etc/hosts ]
```

Many times, even as experienced administrators, we are used to language elements and we accept them as they are. I feel many Linux administrators will be surprised to learn that `[` is a command for both a shell built-in and a standalone file. Using the `type` command we can verify this:

```
$ type -a [
```

We can see the output of this command in the following screenshot confirming its existence:

```
pi@pilabs ~ $ type -a [
[ is a shell builtin
[ is /usr/bin/[
pi@pilabs ~ $
```

We can see that on the Raspbian distribution that I am using, there is the built-in [command and the /usr/bin/[command. As we have seen, both these commands imitate the test command but it requires a closing bracket.

Now we know a little more about the [command, which is found in bash and the earlier Bourne shell; we can now continue to add a little command-line list syntax. In addition to the command-line list, we can see the desired functionality working in the following code sample:

```
$ FILE=/etc/hosts
$ [ -f $FILE -a -r $FILE ] && cat $FILE
```

Having set the parameter FILE variable, we can test that it is both a regular file and is readable by the user before attempting to list the file contents. In this way, the script becomes more robust without the need for a complex script logic. We can see the code in use in the following screenshot:

```
pi@pilabs ~ $ FILE=/etc/hosts
pi@pilabs ~ $ [ -f $FILE -a -r $FILE ] && cat $FILE
127.0.0.1       localhost
::1             localhost ip6-localhost ip6-loopback
fe00::0         ip6-localnet
ff00::0         ip6-mcastprefix
ff02::1         ip6-allnodes
ff02::2         ip6-allrouters

#127.0.1.1      pilabs.theurbanpenguin.com
pi@pilabs ~ $ _
```

This type of abbreviation is quite common and is easily recognizable. We should always be cautious of using abbreviations if they do not add readability. Our aim in scripting should be to write a clear and understandable code and avoid shortcuts if they do not add to this goal.

Providing parameter defaults

Within bash parameters, there are named spaces in the memory that allow us access to stored values. There are two types of parameters:

- Variables
- Special parameters

Special parameters are read-only and are pre-set by the shell. Variables are maintained by ourselves as well as bash. In general, when talking about syntax, bash will refer to variables by their family name of parameters.

Variables

Variables are one type of parameter. These can be set by the system or by ourselves. For example, $USER is a variable parameter that is set by the system but can be written by us. As such, it is not a read-only requisite of special parameters.

Special parameters

Special parameters are the second parameter type and are managed by the shell itself and are presented as read-only. We have come across these before in parameters, such as $0 but let's take a look at another $-. We can expand these parameters to gain an understanding of their use, using the echo command:

```
$ echo "My shell is $0 and the shell options are: $-"
```

From the annotated text that I have added, we can understand that the $- option represents the shell options that are configured. These can be displayed using the set -o command but it can be read programmatically using $-.

We can see this in the following screenshot:

```
pi@pilabs ~ $ echo "I am using $0 with the options: $-"
I am using -bash with the options: himBH
pi@pilabs ~ $
```

The options set here are as follows:

- h: This is hashall that allows for programs to be found using the PATH parameter
- i: This shows that this is an interactive shell
- m: This is short for monitor, which allows the use of the bg and fg commands to bring commands in and out of the background
- B: This allows the brace expansion or mkdirdir{1,2} where we create dir1 and dir2
- H: This allows history expansion or running commands, such as !501 to repeat commands from history

Setting defaults

Using either the `test` command or the brackets, we can provide default values for variables, including command-line parameters. Taking the `hello4.sh` script we worked with earlier, we can modify it and set the `name` parameter if it is zero bytes:

```
#!/bin/bash
name=$1
[ -z $name ] && name="Anonymous"
echo "Hello $name"
exit 0
```

This code is functional but it is our choice how we code in the default value. We can alternatively assign a default value directly to the parameter. Consider the following code, where a default assignment is made directly:

```
name=${1-"Anonymous"}
```

In bash, this is known as **parameter substitution** and can be written in the following pseudo-code:

```
${parameter-default}
```

Wherever a variable (parameter) has not been declared and has a null value the default value will be used. If the parameter has been explicitly declared with a null value, we will use the `:-` syntax, as shown in the following example:

```
parameter=
${parameter:-default}
```

By editing the script now, we can create `hello8.sh` to make use of bash parameter substitution to provide the default value:

```
#!/bin/bash
#Use parameter substitution to provide default value
name=${1-"Anonymous"}
echo "Hello $name"
exit 0
```

This script and its output, both with and without a supplied value, are shown in the following screenshot:

```
pi@pilabs ~ $ hello8.sh
Hello Anonymous
pi@pilabs ~ $ hello8.sh   fred
Hello fred
pi@pilabs ~ $ cat bin/hello8.sh
#!/bin/bash
name=${1-"Anonymous"}
echo "Hello $name"
exit 0
pi@pilabs ~ $ _
```

The `hello8.sh` script provides the functionality that we need with the logic built directly into the parameter assignment. The logic and assignment now are a single line of code within the script and it is a major step in keeping the script simple and maintaining the readability.

When in doubt – Quote!

Having established that variables are a type of parameter, we should always keep this in mind, especially, when reading manuals and HOWTOs. Often the documentation refers to parameters and in doing so they include variables, as well as, the bash special parameters, such as $1 and so on. In keeping with this, we will look at why it is advisable to quote the parameters when we use them on the command line or within scripts. Learning this now can save us a lot of pain and heartache later, especially, when we start looking at loops.

First, the correct term that we should use for reading the value of variables is **parameter expansion**. To you and me this is reading a variable, but to bash this would be too simple. The assignment of a correct name, such as parameter expansion reduces any ambiguity to its meaning but adds complexity at the same time. In the following example, the first line of code assigns the value of fred to the name parameter. The second line of code uses parameter expansion to print the stored value from memory. The $ symbol is used to allow the expansion of the parameter:

```
$ name=fred
$ echo "The value is: $name"
```

In the example, we have used the double quotes to allow `echo` to print the single string as we have used spaces. Without the use of quotes, the echo might have seen this as multiple arguments. The space being the default field separator in most shells including bash. Often, when we do not think to use the quotes, we do not see the spaces directly. Consider the following extract of command-line code that we made use of earlier:

```
$ FILE=/etc/hosts
$ [ -f $FILE -a -r $FILE ] && cat $FILE
```

Even though this worked, we may have been a little fortunate, especially, if we were populating the FILE parameter from a list of files that we had not created ourselves. It is quite conceivable that a file can have spaces within its name. Let's now replay this code using a different file. Consider the following command:

```
$ FILE="my file"
$ [ -f $FILE -a -r $FILE ] && cat $FILE
```

Even though structurally there has been no change to the code, it now fails. This is because we are providing too many arguments to the [command. The failing result will be the same even if we use the `test` command.

Even though we have correctly quoted the assignment of the file name to the parameter FILE, we have NOT protected the spaces when the parameter is expanded. We can see the code failing, as it is captured in the following screenshot:

```
pi@pilabs ~ $ FILE="my file"
pi@pilabs ~ $ [ -f $FILE -a -r $FILE ] && cat $FILE
-bash: [: too many arguments
pi@pilabs ~ $
```

We can see that this will not be ready for our scripts. Alas, what we once thought as robust, is now in tatters and like the Titanic, our code has sunk.

However, a simple solution is to revert to quoting parameter expansion unless, specifically, not desired. We can make this ship unsinkable by a simple edit to the code:

```
$ FILE="my file"
$ [ -f "$FILE" -a -r "$FILE" ] && cat "$FILE"
```

We can now proudly stand on the White Star Line dock, as we see the Titanic II get launched in the following code example, which is captured in the following screenshot:

```
pi@pilabs ~ $ FILE="my file"
pi@pilabs ~ $ [ -f "$FILE" -a -r "$FILE" ] && cat "$FILE"
The File Contents
pi@pilabs ~ $ _
```

It is truly amazing and sometimes just a little unbelievable what affect these tiny quotes can have. We should never ignore the quotes when expanding variables. To ensure that we drill home this point, we can highlight this phenomenon in another even simpler example. Let's take the scenario where we now just want to remove the file. In the first example we do not use quotes:

```
$ rm $FILE
```

This code will produce failures as the parameter expansion will lead to the following perceived command:

```
$ rm my file
```

The code will fail because it is unable to find the `my` file or the `file` file. Even worse, potentially, we could be deleting incorrect files if any of the names could be resolved accidently.

Whereas quoting the parameter expansion will save the day, as we see in the second example:

```
$ rm "$FILE"
```

This is correctly expanded to the desired command that we illustrate in the following code example:

```
$ rm "my file"
```

I certainly hope that these examples demonstrate the need for care when expanding parameters and you are aware of the pit-falls.

Advanced test using [[

The use of the double brackets [[condition]] allows us to do more advanced condition testing but is not compatible with the Bourne Shell. The double brackets were first introduced as a defined keyword in the korn shell and are also available in bash and zsh. Unlike the single bracket, this is not a command but a keyword. The use of the type command can confirm this:

```
$ type [[
```

Whitespace

The fact that [[is not a command is significant where whitespace is concerned. As a keyword, [[parses its arguments before bash expands them. As such, a single parameter will always be represented as a single argument. Even though it goes against best practice, [[can alleviate some of the issues associated with whitespace within parameter values. Reconsidering the condition we tested earlier, we can omit the quotes when using [[,as shown in the following example:

```
$ echo "The File Contents">"my file"
$ FILE="my file"
$ [[ -f $FILE && -r $FILE ]] && cat "$FILE"
```

We still need to quote the parameter when using cat as you can see and we can use quotes within the double brackets but they become optional. Note we can also use the more traditional && and || to represent -a and -o respectively.

Other advanced features

Some of the extra features that we can include with the double brackets. Even if we lose portability in using them, there are some great features that overcome the loss. Remember that if we only use bash then we can use the double brackets but can't run our scripts in the Bourne Shell. The advanced features that we gain which are covered in the following sections include pattern matching and regular expressions.

Pattern matching

Using the double brackets we can do more than just match strings, we can use pattern matching. For example, we may need to work exclusively with Perl scripts, files that end with .pl. We will be able to implement this easily within a condition by including the pattern as a match, as shown in the following example:

```
$ [[ $FILE = *.pl ]] &&cp"$FILE" scripts/
```

Regular expressions

We are not limited to simple pattern matches using the =~ operator, we can additionally match regular expressions. We could rewrite the last example using a regular expression:

```
$ [[ $FILE =~ \.pl$ ]] &&cp "$FILE" scripts/
```

 As the single dot or period has a special meaning in regular expressions, we need to escape it with \.

The following screenshot shows the regular expression matching working with a file called my.pl and another called my.apl. The match correctly shows for the file that ends in .pl:

```
pi@pilabs ~ $ FILE="my.pl"
pi@pilabs ~ $ [[ $FILE =~ \.pl$ ]] && echo "Perl found"
Perl found
pi@pilabs ~ $ FILE="my.apl"
pi@pilabs ~ $ [[ $FILE =~ \.pl$ ]] && echo "Perl found"
pi@pilabs ~ $ _
```

Regular expression script

The power of regular expressions cannot be dismissed. Another simple demonstration of conditional testing using regular expressions will be to expose the US and UK spelling of color: being color and colour. We may prompt the user if they want a color or mono output for the script but at the same time cater for both spellings. The line that will do the work in the script is as follows:

```
if [[ $REPLY =~ colou?r ]] ; then
```

The regular expression caters to both spellings of color by making the u optional: u?. Furthermore, we can disable case sensitivity allowing for *COLOR* and color by setting a shell option:

```
shopt -s nocasematch
```

This option can be disabled again at the end of the script with the following command:

```
shopt -s nocasematch
```

When we use the variable parameters that we have named $GREEN and $RESET we affect the color of the output. The color green will only be shown where we have sourced the color definition file. This is set when we choose the color display. Selecting mono will ensure that the variable parameters are null and have no effect.

The complete script is shown in the following screenshot:

```
#!/bin/bash
# Welcome script to display a message to users on login
# Author: @theurbanpenguin
# Date: 1/1/1971
shopt -s nocasematch #turn off case sensitivity
read -p "Type color or mono for script output: "
if [[ $REPLY =~ colou?r ]] ; then
    source $HOME/snippets/color
fi
#Where parameters are not set the display will be mono
echo -e "${GREEN}This is $0 $RESET"
shopt -u nocasematch #reset case sensitivity
exit 0
```

Arithmetic operations using ((

When using bash and some other advanced shells, we may make use of the (( )) notation to simplify mathematical operations with scripts.

Simple math

The double parenthesis construct in bash allows for arithmetic expansion. Using this in the simplest format, we can easily carry out integer arithmetic. This becomes a replacement for the let built-in. The following examples show the use of the let command and the double parenthesis to achieve the same result:

```
$ a=(( 2 + 3 ))
$ let a=2+3
```

In both cases, the a parameter is populated with the sum of 2 + 3.

Parameter manipulation

Perhaps, a little more useful to us in scripting is the C-style parameter manipulation that we can include using the double parenthesis. We can often use this to increment a counter within a loop and also put a limit on the number of times the loop iterates. Consider the following code:

```
$ COUNT=1

$ (( COUNT++ ))

echo $COUNT
```

Within this example, we first set COUNT to 1 and then we increment it with the ++ operator. When it is echoed in the final line, the parameter will have a value of 2. We can see the results in the following screenshot:

```
pi@pilabs ~/bin $ COUNT=1
pi@pilabs ~/bin $ (( COUNT++ ))
pi@pilabs ~/bin $ echo $COUNT
2
pi@pilabs ~/bin $
```

We can achieve the same result in long-hand by using the following syntax:

```
$ COUNT=1

$ (( COUNT=COUNT+1 ))

echo $COUNT
```

This of course allows for any increment of the COUNT parameter and not just a single unit increase. Similarly, we can count down using the -- operator, as shown in the following example:

```
$ COUNT=10

$ (( COUNT-- ))

echo $COUNT
```

We start using a value of 10, reducing the value by 1 within the double parenthesis.

 Note that we do not use the $ to expand the parameters within the parenthesis. They are used for parameter manipulation and as such we do not need to expand parameters explicitly.

Standard arithmetic tests

Another advantage that we can gain from these double parentheses is with the tests. Rather than having to use `-gt` for greater than we can simply use `>`. We can demonstrate this in the following code:

```
$(( COUNT > 1 )) && echo "Count is greater than 1"
```

The following screenshot demonstrates this for you:

```
pi@pilabs ~/bin $ COUNT=10
pi@pilabs ~/bin $ (( COUNT-- ))
pi@pilabs ~/bin $ (( COUNT > 1 )) && echo "Count is greater than 1"
Count is greater than 1
pi@pilabs ~/bin $
```

It is this standardization, both in the C-style manipulation and tests, that make the double parenthesis so useful to us. This use extends to both, the command line and in scripts. We will use this feature extensively when we look at looping constructs.

Summary

Within this chapter, I really hope that we have introduced many new and interesting choices to you. This was an area with a wide range where we began recapping on the use of test and discovered that the `[` is a command is not a syntax construct. The main effect that it is a command is on whitespace and we looked at the need to quote variables.

Even though we may commonly call variables as variables. We have also seen that their correct name, especially in documentation is parameters. Reading a variable is a parameter expansion. Understanding parameter expansion can help us understand the use of the keyword `[[`. The double square brackets are not commands and do not expand the parameters. This means that we do not need to quote variables even if they do contain whitespace. Moreover, we can use advanced tests with double square brackets, such as pattern matching or regular expressions.

Finally, we looked at arithmetic expansion and parameter manipulation using the double parenthesis notation. The biggest feature this delivers is the possibility to easily increment and decrement counters.

In the next chapter, we will move into the looping constructs found in bash and make use of some of our new found skills from this chapter.

6
Iterating with Loops

Remember, scripts are for lazy people. We are the folk of the world who have better things to do than repeat a task 100 times or more; loops are our friends.

Looping structures are the life-blood of scripts. These loops are the workhorse engine that can iterate many times, repeating the same task reliably and consistently. Imagine having 100,000 lines of text within a CSV file that has to be checked for incorrect entries. A script can do this easily and accurately once developed but in the case of a human, the reliability factor and accuracy will fail very quickly.

So let's see how we can save our time and sanity by covering the following topics in this chapter:

- For loops
- Loop control
- While and until
- Read from file
- Operator menu

For loops

All our looping controls can be simple and we will begin by looking at `for` loops. The word `for` is a keyword in bash and in working it is similar to `if`. We can use the command type to verify this, as shown in the following example:

```
$ type for
for is a shell keyword
```

As a reserved shell keyword, we can use a `for` loop both in scripts and directly at the command line. In this way, we can utilize loops within and without the scripts optimizing the use of the command line. A simple `for` loop is shown in the following example code:

```
# for u in bob joe ; do
useradd $u
echo '$u:Password1' | chpasswd
passwd -e $u
done
```

Within a `for` loop, we read from the list on the right to populate the variable parameter on the left, in this case we will read from the list containing bob and joe into the parameter variable u. Each item from the list is inserted into the variable, one item at a time. In this way, as long as there are items to be processed in the list, the loop will execute until the list is exhausted.

Practically, for us the execution of this loop means that we will:

- Create the user bob
- Set the password for bob
- Expire the password so it will need to be reset on the first login for the user bob

We then loop back and repeat the process for the user joe.

We can view the previous example in the following screenshot; after having gained root access via `sudo -i`, we proceeded to run the loop and create the users:

```
pi@pilabs ~ $ sudo -i
[sudo] password for pi:
root@pilabs:~# for u in bob joe ; do
> useradd $u
> echo "$u:Password1" | chpasswd
> passwd -e $u
> done
passwd: password expiry information changed.
passwd: password expiry information changed.
root@pilabs:~# 
```

The list that is read in the `for` loop can be generated dynamically or statically, as shown in the last example. To create dynamic lists, we could use various globbing techniques to populate the list. As an example, to work with all files in a directory we could use `*`, as shown in the following example:

```
for f in * ; do
stat "$f"
done
```

 When a list is generated, such as with file globbing, we should quote the expansion of the variable parameter. Without the quotes, it is possible that a space will get included that will cause the command to fail. This is what we have seen here in the `stat` command.

In the following examples, we isolate the filenames that begin with `ba*`. We then use the `stat` command to print the inode metadata. The code and output is shown in the following screenshot:

```
pi@pilabs ~/bin $ for f in ba* ; do
> stat "$f"
> done
  File: `backup2.sh'
  Size: 675            Blocks: 8          IO Block: 4096   regular file
Device: b302h/45826d    Inode: 270110     Links: 1
Access: (0755/-rwxr-xr-x)  Uid: ( 1000/     pi)   Gid: ( 1000/     pi)
Access: 2015-07-17 14:00:04.119477594 +0000
Modify: 2015-07-17 14:00:04.119477594 +0000
Change: 2015-07-17 14:00:04.139477463 +0000
 Birth: -
  File: `backup.sh'
  Size: 775            Blocks: 8          IO Block: 4096   regular file
Device: b302h/45826d    Inode: 268466     Links: 1
Access: (0755/-rwxr-xr-x)  Uid: ( 1000/     pi)   Gid: ( 1000/     pi)
Access: 2015-07-04 19:56:11.481438080 +0000
Modify: 2015-07-04 19:56:11.481438080 +0000
Change: 2015-07-04 19:56:11.491438018 +0000
 Birth: -
```

This list can also be generated from the output of another command or a pipeline of commands. For example, if we need to print the current working directory of all logged in users, we could try something similar to the following:

```
$ for user in $(who | cut -f1 -d"") ; do
lsof -u $user -a -c bash | grep cwd
done
```

In the previous example, we can see that the choice of name for the parameter is down to you; we are not limited to a single character and we can use the $username in this example. Using lowercase we will not overwrite the system variable $USER. The following screenshot demonstrates the loop and the subsequent output:

```
pi@pilabs ~/bin $ for user in $(who | cut -f1 -d" ") ; do
> lsof -u "$user" -a -c bash | grep cwd
> done
bash    14935   pi  cwd   DIR  179,2   4096 268409 /home/pi/bin
bash    15140   pi  cwd   DIR  179,2   4096 268409 /home/pi/bin
pi@pilabs ~/bin $
```

The lsof command will list open files, we can search for the files opened by each user in turn and with the bash command as the current working directory.

Working with the scripts that we have created so far, we can create a new script called hello9.sh. If we copy the $HOME/bin/hello2.sh script to the new script, we can edit it to make use of a for loop:

```
#!/bin/bash
echo "You are using $(basename $0)"
for n in $*
do
    echo "Hello $n"
done
exit 0
```

The loop is used to iterate through each command-line argument supplied and greet each user individually. When we execute the script, we can see that we can now display the hello message for each user. This is shown in the following screenshot.

```
pi@pilabs ~/bin $
pi@pilabs ~/bin $ hello9.sh fred bob
You are using hello9.sh
Hello fred
Hello bob
pi@pilabs ~/bin $
```

Although, what we have seen here is still relatively trivial, we should now realize a little of what we can do with scripts and loops. The arguments of this script can be the usernames that we have already used or anything else. If we stick with the usernames, then it will be very easy to create user accounts and set passwords, as we saw earlier.

Controlling the loop

Having entered our loop, we may need to either exit the loop prematurely or perhaps exclude certain items from processing. If we want to process only directories in a listing, rather than every file of any type, then to implement this, we have loop control keywords, such as `break` and `continue`.

The `break` keyword is used to exit the loop processing no more entries, whereas the `continue` keyword is used to stop the processing of the current entry in the loop and resume the processing with the next entry.

Assuming we only want to process directories, we could implement a test within the loop and determine the file type:

```
$ for f in * ; do
[ -d "$f" ] || continue
chmod 3777 "$f"
done
```

Within the loop we want to set permissions including the SGID and Sticky bits, but for the directories only. The * search will return all files, the first statement within the loop will ensure that we only process directories. If the test is done for the current loop, the target fails the test and is not a directory; the `continue` keyword retrieves the next loop-list item. If the test returns true and we are working with a directory then we will process the subsequent statements and execute the `chmod` command.

If we need to run the loop until we found a directory and then exit the loop we can adjust the code so that we can iterate though each file. If the file is a directory then we exit the loop with the `break` keyword:

```
$ for f in * ; do
[ -d "$f" ] &&break
done
echo "We have found a directory $f"
```

Within the following screenshot, we can see the code that I just wrote in action:

```
pi@pilabs ~ $ for f in * ; do
> [ -d "$f" ] && break
> done
pi@pilabs ~ $ echo "We have found a directory: $f"
We have found a directory: bin
pi@pilabs ~ $
```

By working with the same theme, we can print each directory found in the listing using the following code:

```
for f in * ; do
[ -d "$f" ] || continue
dir_name="$dir_name $f"
done
echo "$dir_name"
```

We can achieve a result by processing the loop item only if it is a directory and within the loop. We can work with regular files only using the if test. In this example, we append the directory name to the dir_name variable. Once we exit the loop, we print he complete list of directories. We can see this in the following screenshot:

```
pi@pilabs ~ $ for f in * ; do [ -d "$f" ] || continue
> dir_list="$dir_list $f"
> done
pi@pilabs ~ $ echo "$dir_list"
 bin python_games snippets
pi@pilabs ~ $ _
```

Using these examples and your own ideas, you should now be able to see how you can control loops using the continue and break keywords.

While loops and until loops

When using the for loop we iterate through a list, it's either the one that we create or the one that is dynamically generated. Using the while or until loops, we loop based on the fact that the condition becomes either true or false.

A while loop loops while the condition is true and conversely an until loop will loop while the condition is false. The following command will count from 10 through to zero. Each iteration of the loop printing the variable and then reducing the value by 1:

```
$ COUNT=10
$ while (( COUNT >= 0 )) ; do
echo -e "$COUNT \c"
(( COUNT-- ))
done ; echo
```

We can see the output of this command in the following screenshot; thus, confirming the countdown to zero:

```
pi@pilabs ~ $ COUNT=10
pi@pilabs ~ $ while (( COUNT >= 0 )) ; do
> echo -e "$COUNT \c"
> (( COUNT-- ))
> done ; echo
10 9 8 7 6 5 4 3 2 1 0
pi@pilabs ~ $ _
```

> The use of the \c escape sequence used here allows the suppression of the line-feed normally used with echo. In this way, we can keep the countdown on the single-line of output. I think you will agree that its a nice effect.

The functionality of this loop can be gained using the until loop; just a quick rethink of the logic is required, as we will want to loop until the condition becomes true. Generally, it is a personal choice and the way the logic works best for you about which loop to use. The following example shows the loop written with the until loop:

```
$ COUNT=10
$ until (( COUNT < 0 )) ; do
echo -e "$COUNT \c"
(( COUNT-- ))
done ; echo
```

Reading input from files

Now, it may seem that these loops can do a little more than just count down numbers. We may want to read data in from a text file and process each line. The shell built-in read command that we saw earlier in this book can be used to read a file line by line. In this way, we can use a loop to process each line of a file.

To demonstrate some of these functionalities, we will use a file that contains the server addresses. These could be hostnames or IP addresses. In the following example, we will make use of the IP addresses of Google DNS Servers. The following command shows the contents of the `servers.txt` file:

```
$cat servers.txt
8.8.8.8
8.8.4.4
```

Using the `read` command in the condition of the `while` loop, we can loop as long as we have more lines to read from the file. We specify the input file directly after the `done` keyword. For each line that we read from the file, we can test if the server is up with the command `ping` and if the server is responding, we append it to a list of available servers. This list is printed once the loop closes. In the following example, we can see that we begin to add in as many elements of scripting as we have covered in this book:

```
$ while read server ; do
ping -c1 $server && servers_up="$servers_up $server"
done < servers.txt
echo "The following servers are up: $servers_up"
```

We can verify the operation in the following screenshot, which captures the output:

```
pi@pilabs ~ $
pi@pilabs ~ $ cat servers.txt
8.8.8.8
8.8.4.4
pi@pilabs ~ $ while read server ; do
> ping -c1 "$server" && servers_up-"$servers_up $servers"
> done < servers.txt
PING 8.8.8.8 (8.8.8.8) 56(84) bytes of data.
64 bytes from 8.8.8.8: icmp_req=1 ttl=52 time=25.1 ms

--- 8.8.8.8 ping statistics ---
1 packets transmitted, 1 received, 0% packet loss, time 0ms
rtt min/avg/max/mdev = 25.187/25.187/25.187/0.000 ms
PING 8.8.4.4 (8.8.4.4) 56(84) bytes of data.
64 bytes from 8.8.4.4: icmp_req=1 ttl=52 time=24.9 ms

--- 8.8.4.4 ping statistics ---
1 packets transmitted, 1 received, 0% packet loss, time 0ms
rtt min/avg/max/mdev = 24.950/24.950/24.950/0.000 ms
pi@pilabs ~ $ echo "These servers are up $servers_up"
These servers are up  8.8.8.8 8.8.4.4
pi@pilabs ~ $ _
```

Using this kind of loop, we can start to build extremely practical scripts to process information either fed from the command line or from scripts. It will be very easy to replace the filename that we read with $1 representing a positional parameter passed into the script. Let's return to the `ping_server.sh` script and adjust it to accept the input parameter. We can copy the script to the new $HOME/bin/ping_server_from_file.sh file. Within the script we first test if the input parameter is a file. We then create an output file with a tile that includes the date. As we enter the loop, we append available servers to this file and list the file at the end of the script:

```
#!/bin/bash
# Author: @theurbanpenguin
# Web: www.theurbapenguin.com
# Script to ping servers from file
# Last Edited: August 2015
if [ ! -f"$1 ] ; then
  echo "The input to $0 should be a filename"
  exit 1
fi
echo "The following servers are up on $(date +%x)"> server.out
done
while read server
do
  ping -c1 "$server"&& echo "Server up: $server">> server.out
done
cat server.out
```

We can execute the script now in the following manner:

```
$ ping_server_from_file.sh servers.txt
```

The output from the script execution should be similar to the following screenshot:

```
pi@pilabs ~/bin $ ping_server_from_file.sh servers.txt
PING 8.8.8.8 (8.8.8.8) 56(84) bytes of data.
64 bytes from 8.8.8.8: icmp_req=1 ttl=52 time=24.5 ms

--- 8.8.8.8 ping statistics ---
1 packets transmitted, 1 received, 0% packet loss, time 0ms
rtt min/avg/max/mdev = 24.578/24.578/24.578/0.000 ms
PING 8.8.4.4 (8.8.4.4) 56(84) bytes of data.
64 bytes from 8.8.4.4: icmp_req=1 ttl=52 time=24.5 ms

--- 8.8.4.4 ping statistics ---
1 packets transmitted, 1 received, 0% packet loss, time 0ms
rtt min/avg/max/mdev = 24.521/24.521/24.521/0.000 ms
The following servers are up on 29/08/15
Server up: 8.8.8.8
Server up: 8.8.4.4
pi@pilabs ~/bin $ _
```

Creating operator menus

We can provide a menu to the Linux operators who need limited functionality from the shell and do not want to learn the details of command line use. We can use their login script to launch a menu for them. This menu will provide a list of command selections to choose from. The menu will loop until the user chooses to exit from the menu. We can create a new $HOME/bin/menu.sh script, the basis of the menu loop will be the following:

```
while true
do
......
done
```

The loop we have created here is infinite. The `true` command will always return true and loop continuously; however, we can provide a loop control mechanism to allow the user to leave the menu. To start building the structure of the menu, we will need to echo some text within the loop asking the user for their choice of command. We will clear the screen before the menu is loaded each time and an additional read prompt will appear after the execution of the desired command.

This allows the user to read the output from the command before the screen is cleared and the menu is reloaded. The script will look like the following code at this stage:

```
#!/bin/bash
# Author: @theurbanpenguin
# Web: www.theurbapenguin.com
# Sample menu
# Last Edited: August 2015

while true
do
  clear
  echo "Choose an item: a,b or c"
  echo "a: Backup"
  echo "b: Display Calendar"
  echo "c: Exit"
  read -sn1
  read -n1 -p "Press any key to continue"
done
```

If you execute the script at this stage, there will be no mechanism to leave the script. We have not added any code to the menu selections; however, you can test functionality and exit using the *Ctrl + c* key.

At this stage the menu should look similar to the output shown in the following screenshot:

```
Choose an item: a,b or c
a: Backup
b: Display Calendar
c: Exit
```

To build the code behind the menu selection, we will implement a `case` statement. This will be added in between the two `read` commands, as follows:

```
read -sn1
  case "$REPLY" in
    a) tar -czvf $HOME/backup.tgz ${HOME}/bin;;
    b) cal;;
    c) exit 0;;
  esac
  read -n1 -p "Press any key to continue"
```

We can see the three options that we have added to the case statement, a, b, and c:

- **Option a**: This runs the tar command to back-up the scripts
- **Option b**: This runs the cal command to display the current month
- **Option c**: This exits the script

To ensure that the user is logged out when exiting from their login script, we will run:

exec menu.sh

The exec command is used to ensure that the shell is left after the menu.sh file is complete. In this way, the user never needs to experience the Linux shell. The complete script is shown in the following screenshot:

```bash
#!/bin/bash
# Author: @theurbanpenguin
# Web: www.theurbapenguin.com
# Sample menu
# Last Edited: August 2015

while true
do
  clear
  echo "Choose an item: a,b or c"
  echo "a: Backup"
  echo "b: Display Calendar"
  echo "c: Exit"
  read -sn1
  case "$REPLY" in
    a) tar -czvf $HOME/backup.tgz ${HOME}/bin;;
    b) cal;;
    c) exit 0;;
  esac
  read -n1 -p "Press any key to continue"
done
```

Summary

We have begun to make progress within this chapter. We have been able to join many of the elements that we have previously used into cohesive and functional scripts. Although the focus of this chapter has been on loops, we have used command-line lists, if statements, case statements, and arithmetic calculations.

We opened this chapter describing loops as the workhorse of our scripts and we have been able to demonstrate this with for, while, and until loops. The for loop is used to iterate through elements of a list. The list can be either static or dynamic, with an emphasis on dynamic lists we showed how simply these are created via file globbing or command expansion.

The while and until loops are controlled using conditions. The while loop will loop whilst the supplied condition is true. The until loop will loop until the supplied condition returns true or whilst it returns false. The continue and break keywords are specific to loops and along with exit, we can control the loop flow.

In the next chapter, we will look at modulizing scripts using functions.

7
Creating Building Blocks with Functions

In this chapter, we will dive into the wonderful world of functions. We can look at these as modular building blocks creating powerful and adaptive scripts. By creating functions, we add the code in a single building block isolated from the rest of the script. Focusing on improvements of a single function is a lot easier than trying to improve the script as a single object. Without functions, it is difficult to hone in on problem areas and the code is often repeated, it means that updates need to happen in many locations. Functions are named as blocks of code or scripts within scripts and they can overcome many problems associated with a more complex code.

As we make our way through the chapter, we will cover the following topics:

- Functions
- Passing parameters to functions
- Returning values
- Menu using functions

Introducing functions

Functions are blocks of code that exist in memory as **named elements**. These elements can be created within the shell environment, as well as within the script execution. When a command is issued at the command line, aliases are checked first and following this we check for a matching function name. To display the functions residing in your shell environment, you can use the following code:

```
$ declare -F
```

The output will vary depending on the distribution you are using and the number of functions you have created. On my Raspbian OS, the partial output is shown in the flowing screenshot:

```
pi@pilabs ~ $ declare -F
declare -f __expand_tilde_by_ref
declare -f __get_cword_at_cursor_by_ref
declare -f __git_aliased_command
declare -f __git_aliases
declare -f __git_complete_file
declare -f __git_complete_remote_or_refspec
declare -f __git_complete_revlist
declare -f __git_complete_revlist_file
declare -f __git_complete_strategy
```

Using the -f option, you can display the function and the associated definition. However, if we want to see just a single function definition, we can use the type command:

```
$ type quote
```

The previous code example will display the code block for the quote function, if it exists within your shell. We can see the output of this command in the following screenshot:

```
pi@pilabs ~ $ type quote
quote is a function
quote ()
{
    local quoted=${1//\'/\'\\\'\'};
    printf "'%s'" "$quoted"
}
```

The quote function in bash inserts single quotes around a supplied input parameter. For example, we can expand the USER variable and display the value as a string literal; this is shown in the following screenshot. The screenshot captures the command and output:

```
'pi'pi@pilabs ~ $ quote $USER
'pi'pi@pilabs ~ $
```

Most codes can be represented by a pseudo-code which shows an example layout. Functions are no different and the code to create a function is listed in the following example:

```
function <function-name> {
<code to execute>
}
```

The function is created without a do and done block, as we have used in the previous loops. It is the purpose of the brace brackets to define the code block boundaries.

A simple function to display aggregated system information is shown in the following code. This can be created at the command line and will be a resident in your shell. This will not persist the logins and will be lost when the shell is closed or the function is unset. To allow the function to persist, we need to add this to the login script of our user account. The sample code is as follows:

```
$ function show_system {
echo "The uptime is:"
uptime
echo
echo "CPU Detail"
lscpu
echo
echo "User list"
who
}
```

We can print the detail of the function similar to the prior instance using the type command; this is shown in the following screenshot:

```
pi@pilabs ~ $ type show_system
show_system is a function
show_system ()
{
    echo "The uptime is:";
    uptime;
    echo;
    echo "CPU Detail";
    lscpu;
    echo;
    echo "User list";
    who
}
```

To execute the function, we need to simply type `show_system` and we will see the static text and output from the three commands: `uptime`, `lscpu`, and `who`. This of course is a very simple function but we can start to add more functionality by allowing parameters to be passed at runtime.

Passing parameters to functions

Earlier within this chapter, we referred to functions as scripts within scripts and we will still maintain that analogy. Similar to how a script can have input parameters, we can create functions that also accept parameters that can make their operation less static. Before we work on a script, we can look at a useful function in the command line.

 One of my pet-peeves is over commented configuration files, especially where documentation exists to detail the options available.

The GNU Linux command `sed` can easily edit the file for us and remove commented lines and empty lines. We are introducing the stream editor, `sed`, here but we will look at it in more detail in the following chapter.

The `sed` command line that runs the in-place edit will be:

```
$ sed -i.bak '/^\s*#/d;/^$/d' <filename>
```

We can run out forensics in the command line by breaking it down element by element. Let's take a deeper look:

- `sed -i.bak`: This edits the file and creates a backup with the extension `.bak`. The original file will then be accessible as `<filename>.bak`.

- `/^`: Lines that start with, that is the first character of the line.

- `\s*`: This means any amount of white space including no spaces or tabs.

- `#/`: Followed by the comment. Altogether `/^\s*#/` we are looking for lines that begin with a comment or spaces and a comment.

- `d`: The action delete to remove matching lines.

- `;/^$/d`: The semi-colon is used to separate expressions and the second expression is similar to the first but this time we are preparing to delete empty lines or lines that being with the end of line marker `$`.

To move this into a function, we will simply need to think of a great name. I like to build verbs into function names; it helps with the uniqueness and identifies the purpose of the function. We will create the `clean_file` function as follows:

```
$ function clean_file {
  sed -i.bak '/^\s*#/d;/^$/d' "$1"
}
```

As within scripts, we use positional parameters to accept command-line arguments. We can replace the hard-coded filename that we used previously with `$1` within the function. We will quote this variable to protect against spaces within the filename. To test the `clean_file` function, we will make a copy of a system file and work with the copy. In this way, we can be sure that no harm comes to any system file. We can assure all readers that no system files were harmed during the making of this book. The following are the detailed steps we need to follow to perform the test on the new function:

1. Create the `clean_file` function as described.

2. Move to your home directory using the `cd` command without arguments.

3. Copy the time configuration file to your home directory:
   `cp /etc/ntp.conf $HOME`.

4. Count the number of lines in the file with the following command: `wc -l $HOME/ntp.conf`.

5. Now, remove the commented and empty lines with: `clean_file $HOME/ntp.conf`.

6. Now, recount the lines using: `wc -l $HOME/ntp.conf`.

7. From the backup of the original that we created: `wc -l $HOME/ntp.conf.bak`.

The sequence of commands is shown in the following screenshot:

```
pi@pilabs ~ $ function clean_file { sed -i.bak '/^\s*#/d;/^$/d' "$1"; }
pi@pilabs ~ $ cd
pi@pilabs ~ $ cp /etc/ntp.conf $HOME
pi@pilabs ~ $ wc -l $HOME/ntp.conf
55 /home/pi/ntp.conf
pi@pilabs ~ $ clean_file $HOME/ntp.conf
pi@pilabs ~ $ wc -l $HOME/ntp.conf
13 /home/pi/ntp.conf
pi@pilabs ~ $ wc -l $HOME/ntp.conf.bak
55 /home/pi/ntp.conf.bak
pi@pilabs ~ $ _
```

We can direct the attention of the function to the required file using the argument that was supplied while executing the function. If we need to persist this function, then we should add it to a login script. However, if we want to test this within a shell script, we can create the following file to do this and practice some of the other elements we have learned. We will need to take notice that the functions should always be created at the start of the script as they need to be stored in memory by the time they are called. Just think that your function needs to be unlocked and loaded before you pull the trigger.

We will create a new shell script, $HOME/bin/clean.sh and the execute permission, as always, will need to be set. The code of the script is as follows:

```bash
#!/bin/bash
# Script will prompt for filename
# then remove commented and blank lines

function is_file {
    if [ ! -f "$1" ] ; then
        echo "$1 does not seem to be a file"
        exit 2
    fi
}

function clean_file {
    is_file "$1"
    BEFORE=$(wc -l "$1")
    echo "The file $1 starts with $BEFORE"
    sed -i.bak '/^\s*#/d;/^$/d' "$1"
    AFTER=$(wc -l "$1")
    echo "The file $1 is now $AFTER"
}

read -p "Enter a file to clean: "
clean_file "$REPLY"
exit 1
```

We have provided two functions within the script. The first, is_file, simply tests to ensure that the filename we have entered is a regular file. Then we declare the clean_file function with a little added functionality, displaying the line count of the file before and after the operation. We can also see that functions can be nested and we call the is_file function with clean_file.

Without the function definitions we have only three lines of code at the end of the file that we can see in the example code laid out in the previous code block and has been save as $HOME/bin/clean.sh. We first prompt for the filename and then run the clean_file function, which in turn calls the is_file function. The simplicity of the main code is important here. The complexity is in the functions, as each function can be worked on as a standalone unit.

We can now test the script operation, first using a wrong filename, as we can see in the following screenshot:

```
pi@pilabs ~ $ clean.sh
Enter a file to clean: ntp.cff
ntp.cff does not seem to be a file
pi@pilabs ~ $
```

Now that we have seen the operation with an incorrect file, we can try again using an actual file! We can use the same system file we worked on before. We need to first return the files to their original state:

```
$ cd $HOME
$ rm $HOME/ntp.conf
$ mv ntp.conf.bak ntp.conf
```

With the file now ready, we can execute the script from the $HOME directory as shown in the following screenshot:

```
pi@pilabs ~ $ clean.sh
Enter a file to clean: ntp.conf
The file ntp.conf starts with 55 ntp.conf
The file ntp.conf is now 13 ntp.conf
pi@pilabs ~ $
```

Returning values from functions

Whenever we have statements that are printed on the screen within the function, we can see their result. However, many times we will want the function to populate a variable within the script and not display anything. In this case, we use `return` in the function. This is especially important when we are gaining input from users. We may prefer the case to translate the input to a known case to make the condition testing easier. Embedding the code in a function allows it to be used many times within a script. The following code shows how we can achieve this by creating the `to_lower` function:

```
function to_lower ()
{
    input="$1"
    output=$(tr [A-Z] [a-z] <<<"$input")
return $output
}
```

Stepping through the code we can begin to understand the operation of this function:

- `input="$1"`: This is more for ease than anything else; we assign the first input parameter to a named variable input.

- `output=$(tr [A-Z] [a-z] <<< "$input")`: This is the main engine of the function where the translation from upper case to lower case occurs. The use of the here string operator `<<<` allows us to expand the variable to read in to the contents to the `tr` program. This is a form of input redirection.

- `return$output`: This is how we create the return value.

One use of this function will be within a script that reads the user's input and simplifies the test to see if they choose Q or q. This can be seen in the following extract of code:

```
function to_lower ()
{
    input="$1"
    output=$(tr [A-Z] [a-z] <<< "$input")
return $output
}

while true
do
  read -p "Enter c to continue or q to exit: "
  $REPLY=$(to_lower "$REPLY")
  if [ $REPLY = "q" ] ; then
    break
```

```
    fi

done
echo "Finished"
```

Using functions in menus

In the last chapter, *Chapter 6, Iterating with Loops* we created the `menu.sh` file. Menus are great targets to use functions, as the `case` statement is maintained very simply with single line entries, while the complexity can still be stored in each function. We should consider creating a function for each menu item. If we copy the previous `$HOME/bin/menu.sh` to `$HOME/bin/menu2.sh`, we can improve the functionality. The new menu should look like the following code:

```bash
#!/bin/bash
# Author: @theurbanpenguin
# Web: www.theurbapenguin.com
# Sample menu with functions
# Last Edited: Sept 2015

function to_lower {
    input="$1"
    output=$(tr [A-Z] [a-z] <<< "$input")
return $output
}

function do_backup {
    tar -czvf $HOME/backup.tgz ${HOME}/bin
}

function show_cal {
    if [ -x /usr/bin/ncal ] ; then
      command="/usr/bin/ncal -w"
    else
      command="/usr/bin/cal"
    fi
    $command
}

while true
do
  clear
  echo "Choose an item: a, b or c"
  echo "a: Backup"
```

```
      echo "b: Display Calendar"
      echo "c: Exit"
      read -sn1
      REPLY=$(to_lower "$REPLY")
      case "$REPLY" in
        a) do_backup;;
        b) show_cal;;
        c) exit 0;;
      esac
      read -n1 -p "Press any key to continue"
   done
```

As we can see, we still maintain the simplicity of the case statement; however, we can develop the script to add in more complexity through the functions. For example, when choosing option b for the calendar, we now check to see if the ncal command is available. If it is, we use ncal and use the -w option to print the week number. We can see this in the following screenshot where we have chosen to display the calendar and install ncal.

```
Choose an item: a,b or c
a: Backup
b: Display Calendar
c: Exit
     September 2015
Mo      7 14 21 28
Tu  1   8 15 22 29
We  2   9 16 23 30
Th  3 10 17 24
Fr  4 11 18 25
Sa  5 12 19 26
Su  6 13 20 27
    36 37 38 39 40
Press any key to continue_
```

We can also not be concerned about the caps-lock key as the to_lower function converts our selection to lower case. Over time it would be very easy to add additional elements to the functions knowing that we only affect that single function.

Summary

We are still making progress by leaps and bounds in script writing. I hope these ideas stay with you and you find the code examples useful. Functions are very important for the ease of maintenance of your scripts and their ultimate functionality. The easier the scripts are to maintain, the more likely you are to add improvements over time. We can define functions at the command line or within scripts but they need to be included in the script before they are used.

The functions themselves are loaded in to memory while the script is running, but as long as the script is forked and not sourced, they will be released from memory once the script is finished. We have touched a little upon `sed` in this chapter and we will look more at using the stream editor (`sed`) in the next chapter. The `sed` command is very powerful and we can make good use of it within scripts.

8

Introducing sed

In the previous chapter, we saw that we could make use of sed to edit files from within our scripts. The sed command is the **Stream Editor** and opens the file line by line to search or edit the file contents. Historically, this goes way back to Unix where systems may not have had enough RAM to open very large files. Using sed was absolutely required to carry out edits. Even today, we will use sed to make changes and display data from files with hundreds and thousands of entries. It is simpler and easier and more reliable than a human trying to do the same thing. Most importantly, as we have seen, we can use sed in scripts to edit the files automatically, no human interaction is required.

We will start by looking at grep and search the files for text. The re in grep command is short for **Regular Expression**. This introduces the power of POSIX Compliant Regular Expressions before we look at sed. Even though we are not looking at scripting in this chapter, we will be covering some very important tools that we can use with scripts. In the next chapter, we will see the practical implementation of sed in scripts.

For the moment, we have enough queued and we will cover the following topics in this chapter:

- Using grep to display text
- Using regular expressions
- Understanding the basics of sed

Using grep to display text

Welcome back and welcome to the power of using regular expressions in the command line. We will be beginning this journey by looking at the grep command. This will enable us to grasp some simple concepts of searching through the text before moving onto more complex regular expressions and the editing file with sed.

Global Regular Expression Print (grep), or what we more commonly call the command grep, is a command line tool used to search globally (across all the lines in a file) and print the result to STDOUT. The search string is a regular expression.

The grep command is such a common tool that it has many simple examples and numerous occasions where we can use it each day. In the following section, we have included some simple and useful examples with explanations.

Displaying received data on an interface

In this example, we will print just the received data from the eth0 interface.

This is the interface that is my primary network connection to the Raspberry Pi that we are using in this course. If you are uncertain of your interface name, you can use the ifconfig -a command to display all the interfaces and choose the correct interface name on your system. If ifconfig is not found, try typing the full path /sbin/ifconfig.

Using just the ifconfig eth0 command, a heap of data can be printed to the screen. To show just the packets received, we can isolate the lines that contain RX packets (RX for received). This is where grep comes in:

```
$ ifconfig eth0 | grep "RX packets"
```

Using the pipe or vertical bars we can take the output of the ifconfig command and send it to the input of the grep command. In this case, grep is searching for a very simple regular expression, "RX packet". The search string is case-sensitive, so we need to get this right or use the -i option with grep to run the search as case-insensitive, as shown in the following example:

```
$ ifconfig eth0 | grep -i "rx packets"
```

The case-insensitive search is especially useful when searching for options on a configuration file, which often have a mixed-case.

We can see the result of the initial command in the following screenshot, confirming that we have been able to isolate just the single line of output, as shown:

```
pi@pilabs ~ $ ifconfig eth0 | grep "RX packets"
          RX packets:689830 errors:0 dropped:5 overruns:0 frame:0
pi@pilabs ~ $ __
```

Displaying user account data

The local user account database in Linux is the /etc/passwd file and this is readable by all user accounts. If we want to search for the line that contains our own data, we can use either our own login name in the search or use parameter expansion and the $USER variable. We can see this is the following command example:

```
$ grep "$USER" /etc/passwd
```

In this example, the input to grep comes from the /etc/passwd file and we search for the value of the $USER variable. Again, in this case, it is a simple text but it is still the regular expression, just without any operators.

For completeness, we include the output in the following screenshot:

```
pi@pilabs ~ $ grep "$USER" /etc/passwd
pi:x:1000:1000:,,,:/home/pi:/bin/bash
pi@pilabs ~ $ __
```

We can extend this a little using this type of query as a condition within a script. We can use this to check if a user account exists before trying to create a new account. To keep the script as simple as possible and to ensure that the administrative rights are not required, creating the account will display just the prompt and conditional test in the following command-line example:

```
$ bash
$ read -p "Enter a user name: "
$ if (grep "$REPLY" /etc/passwd > /dev/null) ; then
>   echo "The user $REPLY exists"
>   exit 1
>fi
```

The grep search now makes use of the $REPLY variable populated by read. If I enter the name pi, a message will be displayed and we will exit because my user account is also called pi. There is no need to display the result from grep, we are just looking for a return code that is either true or false. To ensure that we do not see any unnecessary output if the user is in the file, we redirect the output from grep to the special device file /dev/null.

If you want to run this from the command line, you should start a new bash shell first. You can do this by simply typing bash. In this way, when the exit command runs it will not log you out but close the newly opened shell. We can see this happening and the results when specifying an existing user within the following graphic:

```
pi@pilabs ~ $ read -p "Enter a user name: "
Enter a user name: pi
pi@pilabs ~ $ if (grep "$REPLY" /etc/passwd > /dev/null ); then
> echo "The user $REPLY exits"
> exit 1
> fi
The user pi exits
exit
pi@pilabs ~ $ _
```

Listing the number of CPUs in a system

Another really useful feature is that grep can count the matching lines and not display them. We can use this to count the number of CPU or CPU cores we have on a system. Each core or CPU is listed with a name in the /proc/cpuinfo file. We can then search for the text name and count the output; the -c option used is shown in the following example:

```
$ grep -c name /proc/cpuinfo
```

I am using a Raspberry Pi 2 and this has four cores, as shown in the following output:

```
pi@pilabs ~ $ grep -c name /proc/cpuinfo
4
```

If we use the same code on a Raspberry Pi Model B that has a single core, we will see the following output:

```
[pi@black-pearl ~ ]$ grep -c name /proc/cpuinfo
1
[pi@black-pearl ~ ]$
```

We can again make use of this in a script to verify if enough cores are available before running a CPU intensive task. To test this from the command line, we can use the following code that we execute on the Raspberry Pi with just the single core:

```
$ bash
$ CPU_CORES=$(grep -c name /proc/cpuinfo)
$ if (( CPU_CORES < 4 )) ; then
> echo "A minimum of 4 cores are required"
> exit 1
> fi
```

We only run bash at the start to ensure that we are not logged out of the system with the exit command. If this was in a script, this will not be required, as we will exit the script and not our shell session.

By running this on the Model B, we can see the results of the script and also the indication that we do not have the required number of cores:

```
[pi@black-pearl ~ ]$ bash
[pi@black-pearl ~ ]$ CPU_CORES=$(grep -c name /proc/cpuinfo)
[pi@black-pearl ~ ]$ if (( CPU_CORES < 4 )); then
> echo "A minumum a 4 cores are required"
> exit 1
> fi
A minumum a 4 cores are required
exit
[pi@black-pearl ~ ]$
```

If you had a requirement to run this check in more than one script, then you could create a function in a shared script and source the script holding the shared functions within the script that requires to be checked:

```
function check_cores {
  [ -z $1 ] && REQ_CORES=2
CPU_CORES=$(grep -c name /proc/cpuinfo)
if (( CPU_CORES < REQ_CORES  )) ; then
echo "A minimum of $REQ_CORES cores are required"
exit 1
fi
}
```

If a parameter is passed to the function, then it is used as the required number of cores; otherwise, we set the value to 2 as the default. If we define this as a function in the shell on the Model B Raspberry Pi and display the details with the command type, we should see this as shown in the following screenshot:

```
[pi@black-pearl ~ ]$ type check_cores
check_cores is a function
check_cores ()
{
    [ -z $1 ] && REQ_CORES=2;
    CPU_CORES=$(grep -c name /proc/cpuinfo);
    if (( CPU_CORES < REQ_CORES )); then
        echo "A minimum a $REQ_CORES cores are required";
        exit 1;
    fi
}
[pi@black-pearl ~ ]$
```

If we run this on a single-core system and specify the requirement of just the single core, we will see that there is no output when we meet the requirement. If we do not specify the requirement, then it will default to 2 cores and we will fail to meet the requirement and we exit the shell.

We can see the output of the function when run with the argument of 1 and then without arguments, as shown in the following screenshot:

```
[pi@black-pearl ~ ]$ check_cores 1
[pi@black-pearl ~ ]$ check_cores
A minimum a 2 cores are required
exit
[pi@black-pearl ~ ]$
```

We can see how useful even the basics of grep can be within the scripts and how we can use what we have learned to start creating usable modules to add to our scripts.

Parsing CSV files

We will now look at creating a script to parse or format a CSV file. The formatting of the file will add new lines, tabs, and color to the output, so that it is more readable. We can then use grep to display single items from the CSV file. The practical application here is a catalog system based on the CSV files.

The CSV file

The CSV file or list of comma separated values will come from the file tools that we have in a current directory. This is a catalog of products that we sell. The file contents are shown in the following output:

```
drill,99,5
hammer,10,50
brush,5,100
lamp,25,30
screwdriver,5,23
table-saw,1099,3
```

This is just a simple demonstration, so we don't expect too much data but each item in the catalog consists of the following:

- Name
- Price
- Units in stock

We can see that we have a drill which costs $99 and we have five units in stock. If we list the file with `cat` it is not very friendly; however, we can write a script to display the data in a more appealing way. We can create a new script called `$HOME/bin/parsecsv.sh`:

```
#!/bin/bash
OLDIFS="$IFS"
IFS=","
while read product price quantity
do
echo -e "\033[1;33m$product \
        =======================\033[0m\n\
Price : \t $price \n\
Quantity : \t $quantity \n"

done <"$1"
IFS=$OLDIFS
```

Let's works through this file and look at the pertinent steps:

Element	Meaning
OLDIFS="$IFS"	The IFS variable stores the file separator and this is normally a white space. We can store the old IFS so that we can restore it later at the end of the script. Ensuring that we return the same environment once the script is complete, no matter how the script is run.
IFS=","	We set the separator to a comma to match what we need with a CSV file.
while read product price quantity	We enter a while loop to populate three variables that we need: product, price, and quantity. The while loop will read the input file, line by line, and populate each of the variables.
echo ...	The echo command displays the product name in blue with double underscores underneath. The other variables are printed on new lines and tabbed in.
done <"$1"	This is where we read the input file, which we pass as an argument to the script.

The script is shown in the following screenshot:

```
#!/bin/bash
OLDIFS="$IFS"
IFS=","
while read product price quantity
do
    echo -e "\033[1;34m$product \
        ==========================\033[0m\n\
    Price : \t $price \n\
    Quantity : \t $quantity \n"

done < "$1"
IFS=$OLDIFS
```

We can execute the script with the tools catalog file located in the current directory using the following command:

```
$ parsecsv.sh tools
```

To look at how this will display, we can view the partial output from the following screenshot:

```
pi@pilabs ~/bin $ parsecsv.sh tools
drill         ==========================
        Price :            99
        Quantity :         5

hammer        ==========================
        Price :            10
        Quantity :         50

brush         ==========================
        Price :            5
```

We are now starting to get the idea that we have a lot of power at the command line to format files in a more readable way and a plain text file does not need to be plain.

Isolating catalog entries

If we need to search for one entry, then we need more than just one line. The entry is in three lines. So, if we search for the hammer, we need to go to the hammer line and the two lines that follow. We do this using the -A option to grep. We need to display the matching line and two lines after. This will be expressed by the following code:

```
$ parsecsv.sh tool | grep -A2 hammer
```

This is displayed in the following screenshot:

```
pi@pilabs ~/bin $ parsecsv.sh tools  | grep -A2 hammer
hammer            =========================
        Price :              10
        Quantity :           50
pi@pilabs ~/bin $
```

Using regular expressions

So far, we have maintained our use of **regular expressions** (**RE**) to simple text but there is, of course, a lot more to learn from them. Although people may often think that the RE seems like comic book profanity that you may see in a Batman fight, they do have a powerful meaning.

Working with alternate spellings

To start with, let's look at some anomalies in spelling. The word color may be spelled colour or color depending upon if we were working with UK English or US English. This can give rise to issues when searching for the word color, as it may be spelled in two ways. Implementing the following command will return only the first line containing the word color and not the second line:

```
$ echo -e "color\ncolour" | grep color
```

If we need to return both spellings, then we can use an RE operator. We will make use of the ? operator. You should be aware that in an RE the ? operator is not the same as in the shell. In an RE the ? operator means that the previous character is optional. When running RE with extra operators, we may need to run grep -E or egrep for the enhanced RE engine:

```
$ echo -e "color\ncolour" | grep -E 'colou?r'
```

We can see this in operation with a quick look at the following screenshot:

```
[pi@black-pearl ~ ]$ echo -e "color\ncolour" | grep -E 'colou?r'
color
colour
[pi@black-pearl ~ ]$
```

How many words have four consecutive vowels?

This ladies and gentlemen is why REs are so important and they are worth persevering with. We can also think of some fun games or crossword solvers. The more fun we have with REs, the easier they are to use. Many Linux systems include a dictionary file located at /usr/share/dict/words and we will use this file if it exits on your system.

How many words can you think of that have four consecutive vowels? Not sure, then let's search the file with grep and REs:

```
$ grep -E '[aeiou]{5}' /usr/share/dict/words
```

First, you can see that we use the square brackets. These have the same meaning as within the shell and OR the grouped characters, as a list. The resulting search is for the letter a or e or i or o or u. Adding the brace brackets at the end enables multipliers. Having just the number 4 in the braces indicates that we are looking for four vowels consecutive row.

We can see this demonstrated in the following screenshot:

```
pi@pilabs ~/bin $ grep -E '[aeoiu]{4}' /usr/share/dict/words
gooier
gooiest
onomatopoeia
onomatopoeia's
plateaued
plateauing
queue
queue's
queued
queues
queuing
pi@pilabs ~/bin $
```

How cool is this? We will never have unfinished crosswords now and no excuse for losing at Scrabble either.

RE anchors

We have already used RE anchors when removing commented lines and blank lines with the `clean_file` function. The `^` or carat represents the start of the line and the `$` represents the end of the line. If we want to list words that begin with `ante` from the dictionary file, we will write the following query:

```
$ grep '^ante' /usr/share/dict/words
```

The result should show anteater, antelope, antenna, and so on. If we want to query for words that end with `cord` we will use:

```
$ grep 'cord$' /usr/share/dict/words
```

This will print a little less and on my system lists the words accord, concord, cord, discord, and record.

So, even though this only introduces a small amount of what we can achieve with regular expressions, we should appreciate what we can gain from knowing just this small amount.

Understanding the basics of sed

Having built a little foundation, we can now start to look at some of the operations of `sed`. The commands will be supplied with most Linux systems and are core commands.

We will dive directly into some simple examples:

```
$ sed 'p' /etc/passwd
```

The `p` operator will print the matched pattern. In this case, we have not specified a pattern so we will match everything. Printing the matched lines without suppressing STDOUT will duplicate lines. The result of this operation is to print all the lines in the passwd file twice. To suppress STDOUT, we use the `-n` option:

```
$ sed -n 'p' /etc/passwd
```

Brilliant!!We have just reinvented the `cat` command. We can now specifically work with just a range of lines:

```
$ sed -n '1,3 p ' /etc/passwd
```

Now we have reinvented the `head` command, but we can also specify the range in an RE to recreate the `grep` command:

```
$ sed -n '/^root/ p' /etc/passwd
```

We can see this demonstrated in the following screenshot:

```
pi@pilabs ~ $ sed -n '/^root/ p' /etc/passwd
root:x:0:0:root:/root:/bin/bash
pi@pilabs ~ $
```

Substituting command

We have seen the p command for printing the pattern space. We will now look at the substitute command or s. With this command, we can replace one string with another. Again by default, we send the output to the STDOUT and do not edit the file.

To replace the default shell of the user pi, we can use the following command:

```
sed -n ' /^pi/ s/bash/sh/p ' /etc/passwd
```

We continue the earlier instance using the p command to print the matched pattern and use the -n option to suppress STDOUT. We search for lines beginning with pi. This represents the username. We then issue the s command to substitute text in those matched lines. This takes two arguments, the first is the text to search for and the second represents the text used to replace the original. In this case, we look for bash and replace it with sh. This is simple and does work but it may not be reliable in the long term. We can see the output in the following screenshot:

```
pi@pilabs ~ $ sed -n ' /^pi/ s/bash/sh/p ' /etc/passwd
pi:x:1000:1000:,,,:/home/pi:/bin/sh
pi@pilabs ~ $
```

We must emphasize that currently we are not editing the file and just displaying it to the screen. The original passwd file remains untouched and we can run this as a standard user. I mentioned in the previous example that the search may be less than reliable as the string we are searching for is bash. This is very short and perhaps it can be included elsewhere on a matched line. Potentially, someone's last name may be "Tabash", which includes the string bash. We can extend the search to look for /bin/bash and replace it with /bin/sh. However, this introduces another problem, which is, the default delimiter is the forward slash so we will have to escape each forward slash we use in the search and replace string, which is:

```
sed -n ' /^pi/ s/\/bin\/bash/\/usr\/bin\/sh/p ' /etc/passwd
```

This is an option but it is not a tidy option. A better solution is to know that the first delimiter we use defines the delimiters. In other words, you can use any character as a delimiter. Using the @ symbol may be a good idea in this scenario, as it does not appear in either the search or the replace string:

```
sed -n ' /^pi/ s@/bin/bash@/usr/bin/sh@p ' /etc/passwd
```

We now have a more reliable search and a readable command line to work with, which is always a good thing. We replace just the first occurrence on each line of /bin/bash with /bin/sh. If we need to replace more than the first occurrence, we add the g command for global at the end:

```
sed -n ' /^pi/ s@bash@sh@pg ' /etc/passwd
```

In our case, it is not required but it is good to know.

Editing the file

If we want to edit the file we can use the -i option. We will need permissions to work with the file but we can make a copy of the file to work with, so we don't harm any system file or require additional access.

We can copy the passwd file locally:

```
$ cp /etc/passwd "$HOME"
$ cd
```

We finish with the cd command to ensure that we are working in the home directory and the local passwd file.

The -i option is used to run an in-place update. We will not need the -n option or the p command when editing the file. As such, the command is as simple as the following example:

```
$ sed -i ' /^pi/ s@/bin/bash@/bin/sh/ ' $HOME/passwd
```

There will be no output to the command but the file will now reflect the change. The following screenshot shows the command usage:

```
pi@pilabs ~ $ sed -i ' /^pi/ s@bash@sh@pg ' "$HOME/passwd"
```

We should make a backup before we make the change by appending a string directly after the `-i` option and without any spaces. This is shown in the following example:

```
$ sed -i.bak ' /^pi/ s@/bin/bash@/bin/sh/ ' $HOME/passwd
```

If we want to see this, we can reverse the search and replace strings:

```
$ sed -i.bak ' /^pi/ s@/bin/sh@/bin/bash/ ' $HOME/passwd
```

This will set the local `passwd` file to be the same as it was before and we will have a `passwd.bak` with the previous set of changes. This keeps us safe with a rollback option if we need it.

Summary

Another great chapter that you have firmly under your belt and I hope this was really useful to you. Although, we want to concentrate on using `sed`, we started with how powerful `grep` can be both inside and outside our scripts. This led us to the Regular Expressions before taking a look at just a few of the possibilities of `sed`. Although, we have only just touched `sed`, we will start extending this in the next chapter were we will expand upon what we have learned. This will take the form of scripting Apache Virtual Hosts by first extracting commented data from the current configuration, uncommenting and writing it to a template. We can then use the template to create new Virtual Hosts. The workhorse of all these operations will be `sed` and `sed` scripts.

9
Automating Apache Virtual Hosts

Now that we have seen a little of the stream editor, sed, we can put this knowledge into practice. In *Chapter 8*, *Introducing sed*, we became used to some of the capabilities of sed; however, this represents just a small amount of the power enclosed in the editor. In this chapter, we are going to exercise sed a little more and expose ourselves to some practical uses of the tool, especially when using our bash scripts.

In this journey, we will use sed to help us automate the creation of Apache name-based Virtual Hosts. The Apache hosts are practical users of sed that we demonstrated but more importantly, we will use sed to search for selected lines in the main configuration. We will then uncomment those lines and save them as a template. Having created the template, we will create new configurations from it. The concept that we demonstrate with Apache can be applied in many different situations.

We will find that using sed in our shell scripts will allow us to easily extract template data from the main configuration and adjust to the needs of the Virtual Host. In this way, we will be able to extend the knowledge of both sed and shell scripting. In this chapter, we are going to cover the following topics:

- Apache HTTPD Virtual Hosts
- Extracting template information
- Creating hosts automatically
- Prompting during host creation

Apache name-based Virtual Hosts

For the demonstration, we will be working with the `httpd.conf` file from an Apache 2.2 HTTPD Server taken from a CentOS 6.6 host. To be perfectly honest, we are far more interested in the configuration file, as Red Hat or CentOS supply it, than the actual configuration changes that we will make. Our purpose is to learn how we can extract data from the system-supplied file and create a template from it. We can apply this to Apache configuration files or any other text data file. It is the methodology, we are not looking at the actual result.

To have some understanding of what we are trying to do, we must first look at the `/etc/httpd/conf/httpd.conf` file that is shipped with Enterprise Linux 6, that is, CentOS, Red Hat Enterprise Linux, or Scientific Linux. The following screenshot shows the virtual host section of the file that we are interested in:

```
#<VirtualHost *:80>
#       ServerAdmin webmaster@dummy-host.example.com
#       DocumentRoot /www/docs/dummy-host.example.com
#       ServerName dummy-host.example.com
#       ErrorLog logs/dummy-host.example.com-error_log
#       CustomLog logs/dummy-host.example.com-access_log common
#</VirtualHost>
```

Looking at these lines, we can see that they are commented and this is all a part of a monolithic `httpd.conf`. While creating Virtual Hosts, we normally preferred separate configurations for each of our potential Virtual Hosts. We need to be able to extract this data from the main file and at the same time uncomment it. We can then save this uncommented data as a template.

Using this template, we will create new configuration files that represent different named `hosts` that we need to have running on one instance of Apache. This enables us to host `sales.example.com` and `marketing.example.com` on the single server. Both sales and marketing will have their own configuration and websites independent from each other. Additionally, it will also be very easy to add additional sites that we need with the template we create. It becomes the task of the main web server to read the incoming HTTP header requests to the server and direct them to the correct site based on the domain name used.

Our first task then will be to extract the data present between the opening and closing `VirtualHost` tags, uncomment it and save this to a template. This will only need to be done once and will not be a part of our main script to create the Virtual Hosts.

Creating the Virtual Hosts template

As we are not going to test the Virtual Hosts we create, we will make a copy of the httpd.conf file and work with that locally in our home directory. This is a good practice while developing the scripts so as not to impact the working configuration. The httpd.conf file that I am working with should be able to be downloaded with other script resources referred to in the script from the publisher. Alternatively, you can copy it from your Enterprise Linux 6 host with Apache installed. Make sure that the httpd.conf file is copied to your home directory and that you are working in your home directory.

First steps

The very first step in creating the template is to isolate the lines that we need. In our case, this will be the lines included in the sample virtual host definition that we saw in the earlier screenshot. This includes the opening and closing tag for the VirtualHost and everything in between. We can use line numbers for this; however, this probably will not be reliable, as we will need to assume that nothing has changed in the file for the line numbers to be consistent. For completeness, we will show this before moving onto a more reliable mechanism.

First, we will remind ourselves of how we can print the whole file with sed. This is important, as in the next step we will filter the display and show only the lines that we want:

```
$ sed -n ' p ' httpd.conf
```

The -n option is used to suppress the standard output and the sed command within the quotes is p, it is used to display the pattern match. As we have not filtered anything here, the matched pattern is the complete file. If we were to use line numbers to filter, we could add line numbers easily with sed, as shown in the following command:

```
$ sed = httpd.conf
```

From the following screenshot, we can see that in this system we need to work with just lines, from 1003 to 1009; however, I do stress again that these numbers may vary from file to file:

```
1003
#<VirtualHost *:80>
1004
#     ServerAdmin webmaster@dummy-host.example.com
1005
#     DocumentRoot /www/docs/dummy-host.example.com
1006
#     ServerName dummy-host.example.com
1007
#     ErrorLog logs/dummy-host.example.com-error_log
1008
#     CustomLog logs/dummy-host.example.com-access_log common
1009
#</VirtualHost>
```

Isolating lines

To display these lines encased with the tags, we can add a number range to sed. This is easily achieved by adding those numbers to sed, as shown in the following command:

```
$ sed -n '1003,1009 p ' httpd.conf
```

With the range of line specified, we have easily been able to isolate the lines that we required and the only lines that are now displayed are those of the Virtual Host definition. We can see this in the following screenshot, which displays both the command and the output:

```
[root@apache ~]# sed -n '1003,1009 p ' httpd.conf
#<VirtualHost *:80>
#     ServerAdmin webmaster@dummy-host.example.com
#     DocumentRoot /www/docs/dummy-host.example.com
#     ServerName dummy-host.example.com
#     ErrorLog logs/dummy-host.example.com-error_log
#     CustomLog logs/dummy-host.example.com-access_log common
#</VirtualHost>
[root@apache ~]#
```

The issue that we face while hard coding in the line numbers is that we lose flexibility. These line numbers relate to this file and maybe only this file. We will always need to check the correct line numbers in the file that relate to the file we are working with. This could be an issue if the lines were not conveniently at the end of the file and we will have to scroll back to try and locate the correct lines number. To overcome these issues, instead of using line numbers we can implement a search for the opening and closing tags directly.

```
$ sed -n '/^#<VirtualHost/,/^#<\/VirtualHost/p' httpd.conf
```

We are no longer using the starting number and ending number but the more reliable starting regular expression and closing regular expression. The opening regular expression looks for the line that begins with #<VirtualHost. The ending regular expression is searching for the closing tag. However, we need to protect the /VirtualHost with an escape character. By looking at the end RE, we see that it translates to lines that begin with #\/VirtualHost, with the escaped forward slash.

 If you recall from *Chapter 8, Introducing sed*, we specify the lines that begin with a specified character by using the carat (^).

By looking at the following screenshot we can now isolate the required lines more reliably and without knowing the lines numbers. This is more desirable across edited files, which will differ in their line numbering:

```
[root@apache ~]# sed -n '/^#<VirtualHost/,/^#<\/VirtualHost/p' httpd.conf
#<VirtualHost *:80>
#       ServerAdmin webmaster@dummy-host.example.com
#       DocumentRoot /www/docs/dummy-host.example.com
#       ServerName dummy-host.example.com
#       ErrorLog logs/dummy-host.example.com-error_log
#       CustomLog logs/dummy-host.example.com-access_log common
#</VirtualHost>
[root@apache ~]#
```

sed script files

Isolating the lines was only the first step! We still have to uncomment the lines and then save the result as a template. Although we can write this as one single sed command string, we can already see that it will be awkwardly long, difficult to read, and edit. Thankfully, the sed command does have the option to read its commands from an input file often known as a script. We use the -f option with sed to specify the file we want to read as our control. For more details on all of the options of sed, the main page is extensive.

We have already seen that we can correctly isolate the correct lines from the file. So, the first line of the script configures the lines that we will work with. We implement the brace brackets {} to define a code block immediately after the selected lines. A code block is one or more commands that we want to run on a given selection.

In our case, the first command will be to remove the comment and the second command will be to write the pattern space to a new file. The sed script should look like the following example:

```
/^#<VirtualHost/,/^#<\/VirtualHost/ {
s/^#//
wtemplate.txt
}
```

We can save this file as $HOME/vh.sed.

In the first line, we select the lines to work with, as we have previously seen and then open the code block with the left brace. In line 2, we use the substitute command, s. This looks for lines that start with a comment or #. We replace the comment with an empty string. There are no characters or spaces between the middle and end forward slash. In English, we are uncommenting the line but to the code this is replacing the # with an empty string. The final line of code uses the write command, w, to save this to template.txt. To help you see this, we have included the following screenshot of the vh.sed file:

```
/^#<VirtualHost/,/^#<\/VirtualHost/ {
s/^#//
w template.txt
}
```

We can see all of our efforts come to fruition now by ensuring that we are in the same directory as the httpd.conf and vh.sed files that are executing the following command:

```
$ sed -nf vh.sed httpd.conf
```

We have now created the `template.txt` file within our working directory. This is the isolated uncommented text from the `httpd.conf` file. In simple terms, we have extracted the seven correct lines from over 1000 lines of text in milliseconds, removed the comment, and saved the result as a new file. The `template.txt` file is displayed in the following screenshot:

```
[root@apache ~]# cat template.txt
<VirtualHost *:80>
    ServerAdmin webmaster@dummy-host.example.com
    DocumentRoot /www/docs/dummy-host.example.com
    ServerName dummy-host.example.com
    ErrorLog logs/dummy-host.example.com-error_log
    CustomLog logs/dummy-host.example.com-access_log common
</VirtualHost>
[root@apache ~]# 
```

Now, we have a template file that we can begin to work with to create Virtual Host definitions. Even though its Apache that we have been looking at, the same idea of uncommenting the text or removing the first character of selected lines can apply to many situations, so take this as an idea of what `sed` can do.

Automating Virtual Host creation

After having created the template, we can now use this to create Virtual Host configurations. In the simplest terms, we need to replace the `dummy-host.example.com` URL with `sales.example.com` or `marketing.example.com` URL. Of course we have to also create the `DocumentRoot` directory, the directory where the web pages will be and also add some basic content. When we use a script to run through the process nothing will be forgotten and the edits will be accurate every time. The basics of the script will be as follows:

```
#!/bin/bash
WEBDIR=/www/docs
CONFDIR=/etc/httpd/conf.d
TEMPLATE=$HOME/template.txt
[ -d $CONFDIR ] || mkdir -p $CONFDIR
sed s/dummy-host.example.com/$1/ $TEMPLATE > $CONFDIR/$1.conf
mkdir -p $WEBDIR/$1
echo "New site for $1" > $WEBDIR/$1/index.html
```

If we ignore the shebang as the first line, we should know this by now. We can start our explanation in line 2 of the script:

Line	Meaning
`WEBDIR=/www/docs/`	We initialize the WEDIR variable that we store in the path to the directory that will hold the different websites.
`CONFDIR=/etc/httpd/conf.d`	We initialize the CONFDIR variable that we will use to store the newly created Virtual Host configuration file.
`TEMPLATE=$HOME/template.txt`	We initialize the variable that we will use for the template. This should point to the path of your template.
`[ -d $CONFDIR ] \|\| mkdir -p "$CONFDIR"`	On a working EL6 host, this directory will exist and is included in the main configuration. If we are running this as a pure test, then we can create a directory to prove that we can create the correct configurations within the target directory.
`sed s/dummy-host.example. com/$1/ $TEMPLATE >$CONFDIR/$1.conf`	The sed command works as an engine in the script running the search and replace operations. Using the substitute command in sed, we search for the dummy text and replace it with the argument passed to the script.
`mkdir -p $WEBDIR/$1`	Here, we create the correct subdirectory to house the websites for the new Virtual Host.
`echo "New site for $1" > $WEBDIR/$1/index.html`	In this final step, we create a basic holding page for the website.

We can create this script as $HOME/bin/vhost.sh. This is illustrated in the following screenshot. Don't forget to add the execute permission:

```
[root@apache bin]# cat vhost.sh
#!/bin/bash
WEBDIR=/www/docs
CONFDIR=/etc/httpd/conf.d
TEMPLATE=$HOME/template.txt
[ -d $CONFDIR ] || mkdir -p $CONFDIR
sed s/dummy-host.example.com/$1/ $TEMPLATE > $CONFDIR/$1.conf
mkdir -p $WEBDIR/$1
echo "New site for $1" > $WEBDIR/$1/index.html

[root@apache bin]#
```

To create the sales Virtual Host and web page, we can run the script as shown in the following example. We will be running the script directly as the root user. Alternatively, you may choose to make use of the sudo command within the script:

```
# vhost.sh sales.example.com
```

We can now see how easily we can create Virtual Hosts using a well-crafted script. The configuration file for the Virtual Host will be created in the /etc/httpd/ conf.d/ directory and will be named sales.example.com.conf. The file will look similar to the following screenshot:

```
[root@apache bin]# cat /etc/httpd/conf.d/sales.example.com.conf
<VirtualHost *:80>
    ServerAdmin webmaster@sales.example.com
    DocumentRoot /www/docs/sales.example.com
    ServerName sales.example.com
    ErrorLog logs/sales.example.com-error_log
    CustomLog logs/sales.example.com-access_log common
</VirtualHost>
[root@apache bin]#
```

The website content must have been created in the /www/docs/sales.example. com directory. This will be a simple holding page that proves the point that we can do this from the script. Using the following command, we can list the content or the base directory that we use to house each site:

```
$ ls -R /www/docs
```

The -R option allows for the recursive listing. We have used the /www/docs directory purely as this is set in the original Virtual Host definition that we extracted. You may prefer to use /var/www or something similar if working in a live environment rather than creating the new directory at the root of your file system. It will be a simple matter of editing the template that we created and that too could be done with sed at the time of template creation.

Prompting for data during site creation

We can now use the script to create the Virtual Hosts and the content but we have not allowed for any customization other than the Virtual Host name. Of course, this is important. After all it is this Virtual Host name that is used in the configuration itself as well as in setting the website directory and the configuration file name.

It is possible that we could allow additional options to be specified during the Virtual Host creation. We will use sed to insert the data as required. The sed command i is to insert data before the selection and a to append after the selection.

For our example, we will add a host restriction to allow only the local network access to the website. We are more interested in inserting data into the file rather than what we are doing with the specific HTTP configuration file. Within the script that we will be adding read prompts in the script and inserting a Directory block into the configuration.

To try and explain what we are trying to do, we should see something similar to the following when executing the script. You can see this from the text that we are creating for the marketing site and adding in restrictions as to who can access the site:

```
[root@apache bin]# ./vhost2.sh marketing.example.com
Do you want to restrict access to this site? y/n y
Which network should we restrict access to: 192.168.0.0/24
[root@apache bin]#
```

As you can see, we can ask two questions, but if needed, more of them can be added to support customization; the idea being that the additional customization should be accurate and reliable in the same way as the script creation was. You may also choose to elaborate the questions with sample answers, so that the user knows how the network address should be formatted.

To aide script creation, we will copy the original vhost.sh to vhost2.sh. We can tidy up a few items in the script to allow for easier expansion and then add in the additional prompts. The new script will look similar to the following code.

```
#!/bin/bash
WEBDIR=/www/docs/$1
CONFDIR=/etc/httpd/conf.d
CONFFILE=$CONFDIR/$1.conf
TEMPLATE=$HOME/template.txt
[ -d $CONFDIR ] || mkdir -p $CONFDIR
sed s/dummy-host.example.com/$1/ $TEMPLATE > $CONFFILE
mkdir -p $WEBDIR
```

```
echo "New site for $1" > $WEBDIR/index.html
read -p "Do you want to restrict access to this site? y/n "
[ $REPLY = 'n' ] && exit 0
read -p "Which network should we restrict access to: " NETWORK
sed -i "/<\/VirtualHost>/i <Directory $WEBDIR >\
  \n  Order allow,deny\
  \n  Allow from 127.0.0.1\
  \n  Allow from $NETWORK\
\n</Directory>" $CONFFILE
```

> Please note that we are not running too many checks in the script. This is to keep our focus on the elements that we are adding rather than a robust script. In your own environment, once you have the script working the way you want you may need to implement more checks to ensure the script reliability.

As you can see, we have a few more lines. The WEBDIR variable has been adjusted to contains the full path to the directory and in a similar way we have added a new variable CONFFILE, so that we can make a reference to the file directly. If the answer to the first prompt is n and the user wants no additional customization, the script will exit. If they answer anything other than n for No, the script will continue and prompt the network to grant access. We can then use sed to edit the existing configuration and insert the new directory block. This will default to deny access but allow from the localhost and NETWORK variables. We refer to the localhost as 127.0.0.1 in the code.

To simplify the code for better understanding, the pseudo-code will look like the following example:

```
$ sed -i "/SearchText/i NewText <filename>
```

Where SearchText represents the line in the file before which we want to insert our text. Also, NewText represents the new line or lines that will be added before the SearchText. The i command directly following the SearchText dictates that we are inserting text. Using the a command to append will mean that the text we add will be added after the SearchText.

We can see the resulting configuration file for `marketing.example.com,` as we have created it with the additional **Directory** block added in the following screenshot:

```
[root@apache bin]# cat /etc/httpd/conf.d/marketing.example.com.conf
<VirtualHost *:80>
    ServerAdmin webmaster@marketing.example.com
    DocumentRoot /www/docs/marketing.example.com
    ServerName marketing.example.com
    ErrorLog logs/marketing.example.com-error_log
    CustomLog logs/marketing.example.com-access_log common
<Directory /www/docs/marketing.example.com >
  Order allow,deny
  Allow from 127.0.0.1
  Allow from 192.168.0.0/24
</Directory>
</VirtualHost>
```

We can see that we have added the new block above the closing `VirtualHost` tag. In the script, this is the `SearchText` that we use. The **Directory** block we add replaces the `NewText` in the pseudo-code. When we look at it, it appears more complex as we have embedded the new lines with \n and formatted the file for easier reading with the line continuation character \. Again, we have to emphasize that this edit was easy and accurate once the script is created.

For completeness, we include the screenshot of the script `vhost2.sh` in the following screenshot:

```
[root@apache bin]# cat vhost2.sh
#!/bin/bash
WEBDIR=/www/docs/$1
CONFDIR=/etc/httpd/conf.d
CONFFILE=$CONFDIR/$1.conf
TEMPLATE=$HOME/template.txt
[ -d $CONFDIR ] || mkdir -p $CONFDIR
sed s/dummy-host.example.com/$1/ $TEMPLATE > $CONFFILE
mkdir -p $WEBDIR
echo "New site for $1" > $WEBDIR/index.html
read -p "Do you want to restrict access to this site? y/n "
[ $REPLY = 'n' ] && exit 0
read -p "Which network should we restrict access to: " NETWORK
sed -i "/<\/VirtualHost>/i <Directory $WEBDIR >\
  \n  Order allow,deny\
  \n  Allow from 127.0.0.1\
  \n  Allow from $NETWORK\
\n</Directory>" $CONFFILE
```

Summary

In this chapter, we have seen how we can extend `sed` into some very cool scripts that have allowed us to extract data from files, uncomment selected lines and write new configurations. Not stopping at that we also saw how we could use `sed` with script that inserts new lines into existing files. I thought that `sed` will very quickly become your friend and we have created some powerful scripts to support the learning experience.

You may already know this but `sed` has a big brother `awk`. In the next chapter, we are going to see how we can use `awk` to extract data from files.

10
Awk Fundamentals

The stream editor is not alone in its family and has a big brother awk. In this chapter, we will run through the basics or fundamentals of awk and see the power of the awk programming language. We will learn why we need and love awk and how we can make use of some of the basic features before we start putting awk to practical use in the next two chapters. As we work our way through this, we will cover the following topics:

- Filtering content from files
- Formatting output
- Displaying non-system users from /etc/passwd
- Using awk control files

The history behind awk

The awk command is a mainstay in the command suite in both Unix and Linux. The Unix command awk was first developed by Bell Labs in the 1970's and is named after the surnames of the main authors: Alfred Aho, Peter Weinberger, and Brian Kernighan. The awk command allows access to the awk programming language, which is designed to process data within text streams.

To demonstrate the programming language that is provided with awk, we should create a hello world program. We know this is compulsory for all languages:

```
$ awk 'BEGIN { print "Hello World!" }'
```

Not only can we see that this code will print the ubiquitous hello message, we can also generate header information with the BEGIN block. Later, we will see that we can create summary information with an END code block by allowing for a main code block.

We can see the output of this basic command in the following screenshot:

```
pi@pilabs ~ $ awk ' BEGIN { print "Hello World!" } '
Hello World!
pi@pilabs ~ $ _
```

Displaying and filtering content from files

Now of course we all want to be able to print a little more than just **Hello World**. The awk command can be used to filter content from files and if needed, very large files. We should begin by printing the complete file before filtering it. In this way, we will get a feel of the syntax of the command. Later, we will see how we can add this control information into awk files to ease the command line. Using the following command, we will print all the lines from the /etc/passwd file:

```
$ awk ' { print } ' /etc/passwd
```

This is equivalent to using the $0 variable with the print statement:

```
$ awk ' { print $0 }' /etc/passwd
```

The $0 variable refers to the complete line. If there is no argument supplied to the print command, we assume that the complete line is to be printed. If we want to print just the first field from the /etc/passwd file, we can use the $1 variable. However, we will need to specify that in this file the field separator used is a colon. The awk default delimiter is a space or any amount of spaces or tabs and newlines. There are two ways to specify the input delimiter; these are displayed in the following examples.

The first example is easy and simple to use. The -F option works well, especially where we do not need any additional header information:

```
$ awk -F":" '{ print $1 }' /etc/passwd
```

We could also do this within the BEGIN block; this is useful when we want to use the BEGIN block to display header information:

```
$ awk ' BEGIN { FS=":" } { print $1 } ' /etc/passwd
```

We can see this clearly in the preceding example, which we named the BEGIN block and all of the code within it is corralled by the brace brackets. The main block has no name and is enclosed within the brace brackets.

After seeing the BEGIN block and the main code blocks, we will now look at the END code block. This is often used to display summary data. For example, if we want to print the total lines in the passwd file, we can make use of the END block. The code with the BEGIN and END blocks is processed just once, whereas the main block is processed for each line. The following example adds to the code we have written so far to include the total line count:

```
$ awk ' BEGIN { FS=":" } { print $1 } END { print NR } ' /etc/passwd
```

The awk internal variable NR maintains the number of processed lines. If we want, we can add some additional text to this. This can be used to annotate the summary data. We can also make use of the single quotes that are used with the awk language; they will allow us to spread the code across multiple lines. Once we have opened the single quotes, we can add new lines to the command line right until we close the quote. This is demonstrated in the next example where we have extended the summary information:

```
$ awk ' BEGIN { FS=":" }
> { print $1 }
> END { print "Total:",NR } ' /etc/passwd
```

If we do not wish to end our awk experience here, we can easily display the running line count with each line as well as the final total. This is shown in the following example:

```
$ awk ' BEGIN { FS=":" }
> { print NR,$1 }
> END { print "Total:",NR } ' /etc/passwd
```

The following screenshot captures this command and partial output:

```
pi@pilabs ~ $ awk ' BEGIN { FS=":" }
{ print NR,$1 }
END { print "Total:",NR } ' /etc/passwd
1 root
2 daemon
3 bin
4 sys
5 sync
```

In the first example with BEGIN, we saw that there is no reason why we cannot use the END code block in isolation without a main code block. If we need to emulate the wc -l command, we can use the following awk statement:

```
$ awk ' END { print NR }' /etc/passwd
```

The output will be the line count from the file. The following screenshot shows both the use of the awk command and the wc command to count the lines in the /etc/passwd file:

```
pi@pilabs ~ $ awk ' END { print NR } ' /etc/passwd
28
pi@pilabs ~ $ wc -l /etc/passwd
28 /etc/passwd
```

Remarkably, we can see that the output does tally to 28 lines and our code has worked.

Another feature that we can practice with is about working on selected lines only. For example, if we want to print only the first five lines, we will use the following statement:

```
$ awk ' NR < 6 ' /etc/passwd
```

If we want to print lines 8 through to 12, we can use the following code:

```
$ awk ' NR==8,NR==12 ' /etc/passwd
```

We can also use regular expressions to match the text in the lines. Take a look at the following example where we look at the lines that end in the work bash:

```
$ awk ' /bash$/ ' /etc/passwd
```

The example and the output it produces is shown in the following screenshot:

```
pi@pilabs ~ $ awk '/bash$/ ' /etc/passwd
root:x:0:0:root:/root:/bin/bash
pi:x:1000:1000:,,,:/home/pi:/bin/bash
bob:x:1001:1004::/home/bob:/bin/bash
joe:x:1002:1005::/home/joe:/bin/bash
pi@pilabs ~ $ _
```

Formatting output

We have remained faithful to the `print` command so far, as we have been limited in what we require from the output. If we want to print out, say, the username, UID, and default shell we need to start formatting the output just a little. In this case, we can organize the output in well-shaped columns. Without formatting, the command we use will look similar to the following example where we use commas to separate the field that we want to print:

```
$ awk ' BEGIN { FS=":" } { print $1,$3,$7 } ' /etc/passwd
```

We use the `BEGIN` block here, as we can make use of it to print column headers later.

To understand the problem a little better, we can take a look at the following screenshot that illustrates the uneven column widths:

```
pi@pilabs ~ $ awk ' BEGIN { FS=":" } { print $1,$3,$7 } ' /etc/passwd
root 0 /bin/bash
daemon 1 /bin/sh
bin 2 /bin/sh
sys 3 /bin/sh
sync 4 /bin/sync
```

The issue that we have in the output is that the columns do not align, as the username is of an inconsistent length. To improve on this, we can use the `printf` function where we can specify the column width. The syntax for the `awk` statements will be similar to the following example:

```
$ awk ' BEGIN { FS=":" }
> { printf "%10s %4d %17s\n",$1,$3,$7 } ' /etc/passwd
```

The `printf` formatting is included within double quotes. We also need to include the newline with the `\n`. The `printf` function does not add a new line automatically, whereas the `print` function does. We print the three fields; the first accepts string values and is set to `10` characters wide. The middle field accepts up to 4 numbers and we finish with the default shell field where we allow up to `17` string characters.

The following screenshot shows how the output can be improved:

```
pi@pilabs ~ $ awk ' BEGIN { FS=":" }
{ printf "%10s %4d %17s\n",$1,$3,$7 } ' /etc/passwd
      root      0       /bin/bash
    daemon      1         /bin/sh
       bin      2         /bin/sh
       sys      3         /bin/sh
      sync      4       /bin/sync
     games      5         /bin/sh
       man      6         /bin/sh
```

We can further enhance this by adding header information. Although the code starts to look untidy at this stage, we will later see how we can resolve this with awk control files. The following example shows the header information being added to the Begin block. The semi-colon is used to separate the two statements in the BEGIN block:

```
$ awk 'BEGIN {FS=":" ; printf "%10s %4s %17s\n","""Name","UID","Shell"}
> { printf "%10s %4d %17s\n",$1,$3,$7 } ' /etc/passwd
```

In the following screenshot, we can see how this improves the output even further:

```
pi@pilabs ~ $ awk 'BEGIN {FS=":";printf "%10s %4s %17s\n","Name","UID","Shell" }
{ printf "%10s %4d %17s\n",$1,$3,$7 } ' /etc/passwd
      Name   UID          Shell
      root      0      /bin/bash
    daemon      1        /bin/sh
       bin      2        /bin/sh
       sys      3        /bin/sh
```

In the previous chapter, we saw how we can augment the output with the use of colors in the shell. We may also use color from within awk by adding our own functions. In the next code example, you will see that awk allows for us to define our own functions to facilitate more complex operations and isolate the code. We will now modify the previous code to include green output in the header:

```
$ awk 'function green(s) {
> printf "\033[1;32m" s "\033[0m\n"
> }
> BEGIN {FS=":" ; green("   Name:  UID:    Shell:"}
> { printf "%10s %4d %17s\n",$1,$3,$7 } ' /etc/passwd
```

Creating the function within awk allows the color to be added where we require, in this case, green text. It will be easy to create functions to define other colors. The code and output is included in the following screenshot:

```
pi@pilabs ~ $ awk 'function green(s) {
printf "\033[1;32m" s "\033[0m\n"
}
BEGIN {FS=":";
green("    Name:    UID:    Shell:") }
{ printf "%10s %4d %17s\n",$1,$3,$7 } ' /etc/passwd
      Name:     UID:      Shell:
       root    0          /bin/bash
     daemon    1          /bin/sh
        bin    2          /bin/sh
        sys    3          /bin/sh
```

Further filtering to display users by UID

We have been able to build our skills with awk piece by piece and what we have learned has been useful. We can take these tiny steps and add them to start creating something a little more usable. Perhaps, we want to print just the standard users; these are usually users higher than 500 or 1000 depending on your particular distribution.

On the Raspbian distribution that I am using for this book, standard users start with UID 1000. The UID is the third field. This is really a simple matter of using the value of the third field as the range operator. We can see this in the following example:

```
$ awk -F":" '$3 > 999 ' /etc/passwd
```

We can show users with UID 101 with the following command:

```
$ awk -F":" '$3 < 101 ' /etc/passwd
```

These just give you an idea of some of the possibilities available with awk. The reality is that we can play all day with our arithmetic comparison operators.

We have also seen that with some of these examples, the awk statements become a little long. This is where we can implement the awk control files. Let's take a look at these straight away before we get lost in a mix of syntax.

Awk control files

Just as with sed, we can simplify the command line by creating and including control files. This also makes the later editing of the command more easily achievable. The control files contain all the statements that we want awk to execute. The main thing that we must consider with sed, awk, and, shell scripts is modularization; creating reusable elements that can be used to isolate and reuse the codes. This saves us time and work and we get more time for the tasks that we enjoy.

To see an example of an awk control file, we should revisit the formatting of the passwd file. Creating the following file will encapsulate the awk statements:

```
function green(s) {
    printf "\033[1;32m" s "\033[0m\n"
}
BEGIN {
    FS=":"
    green("    Name:   UID:       Shell:")
}
{
    printf "%10s %4d %17s\n",$1,$3,$7
}
```

We can save this file as passwd.awk.

Being able to encompass all the awk statements in the one file is very convenient and the execution becomes clean and tidy:

$ awk -f passwd.awk /etc/passwd

This certainly encourages more complex awk statements and allows you to extend more functionality to your code.

Summary

I am hoping that you have a better and clearer understanding of what you can use the awk tool for. This is a data-processing tool that runs through text files, line by line, and processes the code you add. The main block is run for each line that matches the row criteria, if it has been added. Whereas, the BEGIN and END block code is executed just once.

In the next two chapters, we will continue working with awk and some practical examples of how awk is used in real life.

11

Summarizing Logs with Awk

One of the tasks that awk is really good at is filtering data from log files. These log files may be many lines in length, perhaps 250,000 or more. I have worked with data with over a millions lines. Awk can process these lines quickly and effectively. As an example, we will work with a web server access log with 30,000 lines to show how effective and well written awk code can be. As we work our way through the chapter, we will also see different log files and review some of the techniques that we can employ with the awk command and the awk programming language to help with the reporting and administration of our services. In this chapter we will cover the following topics:

- HTTPD log file format
- Displaying data from web server logs
- Summarizing HTTP access codes
- Displaying the highest ranking client IP addresses
- Listing browser data
- Working with e-mail logs

The HTTPD log file format

When working with any a file, the first task is to become familiar with the file schema. In simple terms, we need to know what is represented by each field and what is used to delimit the fields. We will be working with the access log file from an Apache HTTPD web server. The location of the log file can be controlled from the httpd.conf file. The default log file location on a Debian based system is /var/log/apache2/access.log; other systems may use the httpd directory in place of apache2.

To demonstrate the layout of the file, I have installed a brand new instance of Apache2 on an Ubuntu 15.10 system. Once the web server was installed, we made a single access from the Firefox browser to the server from the local host.

Using the `tail` command we can display the content of the log file. Although, to be fair, the use of `cat` will do just as well with this file, as it will have just a few lines:

```
# tail /var/log/apache2/access.log
```

The output of the command and the contents of the file are shown in the following screenshot:

```
root@andrew-15-10:~# tail /var/log/apache2/access.log
127.0.0.1 - - [12/Oct/2015:09:48:42 +0100] "GET / HTTP/1.1" 200 3525 "-" "Mozilla/5.0 (X11; Ubuntu; L
inux x86_64; rv:41.0) Gecko/20100101 Firefox/41.0"
127.0.0.1 - - [12/Oct/2015:09:48:43 +0100] "GET /icons/ubuntu-logo.png HTTP/1.1" 200 3689 "http://loc
alhost/" "Mozilla/5.0 (X11; Ubuntu; Linux x86_64; rv:41.0) Gecko/20100101 Firefox/41.0"
127.0.0.1 - - [12/Oct/2015:09:48:43 +0100] "GET /favicon.ico HTTP/1.1" 404 500 "-" "Mozilla/5.0 (X11;
 Ubuntu; Linux x86_64; rv:41.0) Gecko/20100101 Firefox/41.0"
127.0.0.1 - - [12/Oct/2015:09:48:43 +0100] "GET /favicon.ico HTTP/1.1" 404 500 "-" "Mozilla/5.0 (X11;
 Ubuntu; Linux x86_64; rv:41.0) Gecko/20100101 Firefox/41.0"
```

The output does wrap a little onto the new lines but we do get a feel of the layout of the log. We can also see that even though we feel that we access just one web page, we are in fact accessing two items: the `index.html` and the `ubuntu-logo.png`. We also failed to access the `favicon.ico` file. We can see that the file is space separated. The meaning of each of the fields is laid out in the following table:

Field	Purpose
1	Client IP address.
2	Client identity as defined by RFC 1413 and the `identd` client. This is not read unless `IdentityCheck` is enabled. If it is not read the value will be with a hyphen.
3	The user ID of the user authentication if enabled. If authentication is not enabled the value will be a hyphen.
4	The date and time of the request in the format of `day/month/year:hour:minute:second offset`.
5	The actual request and method.
6	The return status code, such as 200 or 404.
7	File size in bytes.

Even though these fields are defined by Apache, we have to be careful. The time, date, and time-zone is a single field and is defined within square braces; however, there are additional spaces inside the field between that data and the time-zone. To ensure that we print the complete time field if required, we need to print both $4 and $5. This is shown in the following command example:

```
# awk ' { print $4,$5 } ' /var/log/apache2/access.log
```

We can view the command and the output it produces in the following screenshot:

```
root@andrew-15-10:~# awk ' { print $4, $5 } ' /var/log/apache2/access.log
[12/Oct/2015:09:48:42 +0100]
[12/Oct/2015:09:48:43 +0100]
[12/Oct/2015:09:48:43 +0100]
[12/Oct/2015:09:48:43 +0100]
```

Displaying data from web logs

We have already had a preview of how we can use awk to view the logs files from the Apache web server; however, we will now move onto our demonstration file that has a greater and more varied content.

Selecting entries by date

Having seen how we can display the date, we should perhaps look at how we print entries from just one day. To do this, we can use the match operator in awk. This is denoted by the tilde or squiggly line, if you prefer. As we only need the date element, there is no need for us to use both the date and time-zone field. The following command shows how to print entries from 10th September 2014:

```
$ awk ' ( $4 ~ /10\/Sep\/2014/ ) ' access.log
```

For completeness, this command and partial output is shown in the following screenshot:

```
pi@pilabs ~/bin $ awk '( $4 ~ /10\/Sep\/2014/ )' access.log   | less
128.252.139.84 - - [10/Sep/2014:00:00:03 +0100] "GET /wp/?cat=281 HTTP/1.1" 200
51860 "http://theurbanpenguin.com/wp/?cat=281" "Mozilla/5.0 (Macintosh; Intel Ma
c OS X 10_8_5) AppleWebKit/537.36 (KHTML, like Gecko) Chrome/36.0.1985.125 Safar
i/537.36"
41.150.168.184 - - [10/Sep/2014:00:00:23 +0100] "GET /scripting/java.html HTTP/1
```

The round brackets or parentheses embrace the range of lines that we are looking for and we have omitted the main block, which ensures that we print the complete matching lines from the range. There is nothing stopping us from further filtering on the fields to print from the matching lines. For example, if we want to print out just the client IP address that is being used to access the web server we can print field 1. This is shown in the following command example.

```
$ awk ' ( $4 ~ /10\/Sep\/2014/ ) { print $1 } ' access.log
```

If we want to be able to print the total number of accesses on a given date, we could pipe the entries through to the wc command. This is demonstrated in the following:

```
$ awk ' ( $4 ~ /10\/Sep\/2014/ ) { print $1 } ' access.log | wc -1
```

However, if we want to use awk to do this for us, this will be more efficient than starting a new process and we can count the entries. If we use the built-in variable NR, we can print entire lines in the files not just those within the range. It is best to increment our own variable in the main block than matching the range for each line. The END block can be implemented to print the count variable we use. The following command line acts as an example:

```
$ awk ' ( $4 ~ /10\/Sep\/2014/ ) { print $1; COUNT++ }  END { print COUNT }' access.log
```

```
$ awk '( $4 ~ /10\/Sep\/2014/ ) { print $1; COUNT++ } END { print COUNT } ' access.log
```

The output of the count from both wc and the internal counter will give us 16205 as a result from the demonstration file. We should use the variable increment within the main block if we want to count and nothing else.

```
$ awk ' ( $4 ~ /10\/Sep\/2014/ ) { COUNT++ }  END { print COUNT }' access.log
```

We can see this in the following output:

```
pi@pilabs ~/bin $ awk '( $4 ~ /10\/Sep\/2014/ ) { COUNT++ } END { print COUNT } ' access.log
16205
pi@pilabs ~/bin $ _
```

Summarizing 404 errors

The status code of the request page is shown in field 9 of the log. The 404 status will represent the page not found error on the server, I am sure we have all seen that in our browsers at some stage. This may be indicative of a misconfigured link on your site or just produced by a browser searching for the icon image to display in tabbed browsers for the page. You can also identify potential threats to your site by requests looking for standard pages that may give an access to additional information on PHP driven sites, such as WordPress.

Firstly, we can solely print the status of the request:

```
$ awk '{ print $9 } ' access.log
```

We can now extend the code a little as well as ourselves and just print the 404 errors:

```
$ awk ' ( $9 ~ /404/ ) { print $9 } ' access.log
```

This is shown in the following code:

```
pi@pilabs ~/bin $ awk ' ( $9 ~ /404/ ) { print $9 } ' access.log _
```

We can extend this a little further by printing both the status code and the page that was being accessed. This will need us to print field 9 and field 7. Simply put, this will be as shown in the following code:

```
$ awk ' ( $9 ~ /404/ ) { print $9, $7 } ' access.log
```

Many of these failed accessed pages will be duplicated. To summarize these records, we can use the command pipeline to achieve this with sort and uniq commands:

```
$ awk ' ( $9 ~ /404/ ) { print $9, $7 } ' access.log | sort | uniq
```

To use the uniq command, the data must be pre-sorted; hence, we use the sort command to prepare the data.

Summarizing HTTP access codes

It is time for us to leave the pure command line and start working with the awk control files. As always, when the complexity of the required result set increases, we see an increase in the complexity of the awk code. We will create a status.awk file in our current directory. The file should look similar to the following file:

```
{ record[$9]++ }
END {
for (r in record)
print r, " has occurred ", record[r], " times." }
```

First, we will strip down the main code block and this is very simple and sparse. This is a simple way to count each unique occurrence of a status code. Instead of using a simple variable, we feed this into an array. The array in this case is called a record. An array is a multi-values variable and the slots in the array are known as keys. So we will have a collection of variables stored in the array. For example, we expect to see entries for record[200] and record[404]. We populate each key with their occurrence count. Each time we find a 404 code, we increment the count that is stored in the associated key:

```
{ record[$9]++ }
```

In the END block, we create the summary information using a for loop to print out each key and value from the array:

```
END {
for (r in record)
print r, " has occurred ", record[r], " times." }
```

To run this, the associated command line will be similar to the following:

```
$ awk -f status.awk access.log
```

To view the command and output, we have included the following screenshot:

```
pi@pilabs ~/bin $ awk -f status.awk access.log
200  has occurred  23825  times.
206  has occurred  48  times.
301  has occurred  60  times.
302  has occurred  21  times.
304  has occurred  2273  times.
403  has occurred  133  times.
404  has occurred  4382  times.
501  has occurred  63  times.
pi@pilabs ~/bin $
```

We can take this further and focus on the 404 errors. You could, of course, choose any of the status codes. We can see from the results that we have 4382 404 status codes. To summarize these 404 codes, we will copy the status.awk to a new file named 404.awk. We can edit the 404.awk adding an if statement to work only on the 404 codes. The file should be similar to the following code:

```
{ if ( $9 == "404" )
    record[$9,$7]++ }
END {
for (r in record)
print r, " has occurred ", record[r], " times." }
```

If we execute the code with the following command:

```
$ awk -f 404.awk access.log
```

The output will be similar to the following screenshot:

```
pi@pilabs ~/bin $ awk -f 404.awk access.log
404/old/wp-admin/  has occurred  2  times.
404/monitor.html  has occurred  1  times.
404/windows.html  has occurred  1  times.
404/novell.html  has occurred  1  times.
404/user/  has occurred  2  times.
404/linux.html  has occurred  1  times.
404/zcm10.html  has occurred  1  times.
```

Displaying the highest ranking IP address

You should now realize some powers of awk and how immense the language structure is in itself. The data we have been able to produce from the 30K line file is truly powerful and easily extracted. We just need to replace the field we have used before with $1. This field represents the client IP address. If we make use of the following code, we will be able to print each IP Address and also the number of times it has been used to access the web server:

```
{ ip[$1]++ }
END {
for (i in ip)
print i, " has accessed the server ", ip[i], " times." }
```

We want to be able to extend this to show only the highest ranking of IP address, the address that has been used the most to access the site. The work, again, will mainly be in the END block and will make use of a comparison against the current highest ranking address. The following file can be created and saved as ip.awk:

```
{ ip[$1]++ }
END {
for (i in ip)
    if ( max < ip[i] ) {
        max = ip[i]
        maxnumber = i }

print i, " has accessed ", ip[i], " times." }
```

We can see the output of the command in the following screenshot. Part of the client IP address has been obscured as it is from my public web server:

```
pi@pilabs ~/bin $
pi@pilabs ~/bin $ awk -f ip.awk access.log
121.  .52.100  has accessed  12  times.
pi@pilabs ~/bin $ _
```

The functionality of the code comes from within the END block. On entering the END block, we run into a for loop. We iterate through each entry in the ip array. We use the conditional if statement to see if the current value that we are iterating through is higher than the current maximum. If it is, this becomes the new highest entry. When the loop has finished, we print the IP address that has the highest entry.

Displaying the browser data

The browser that is used to access the web site is contained within the log file in field 12. It may be interesting to display the list of browsers used to access your site. The following code will assist you in displaying the list of accesses by the reported browser:

```
{ browser[$12]++ }
END {
    for ( b in browser )
        print b, " has accessed ", browser[b], " times."
}
```

You can see how we can create little plugins to awk with these files and adjust the field and array names to suit your own liking. The output is shown in the following screenshot:

```
pi@pilabs ~/bin $ awk -f browser.awk access.log
"DoCoMo/2.0 has accessed  7  times.
"com.apple.WebKit.WebContent/10600.1.15  has accessed  4  times.
"Xenu  has accessed  3  times.
"-"  has accessed  90  times.
"PHP/5.3.14"  has accessed  1  times.
"FeedBot"  has accessed  8  times.
"OpenOffice/4.1.0"  has accessed  91  times.
"facebookexternalhit/1.1  has accessed  11  times.
""Mozilla/5.0  has accessed  7  times.
"Feed  has accessed  48  times.
"msnbot-UDiscovery/2.0b  has accessed  9  times.
"Twitterbot/1.0"  has accessed  94  times.
"AdsBot-Google  has accessed  10  times.
"Python-urllib/1.17"  has accessed  1  times.
"HTTP_Request2/2.1.1  has accessed  4  times.
"Mozilla/4.0  has accessed  1713  times.
```

Interestingly, we see that the Mozilla 4 and 5 make up the majority of the requesting client. We see that Mozilla 4 is listed here **1713** times. The Mozilla/5.0 entry here is malformed with an extra double-quote. It appears later with 27K accesses.

Working with e-mail logs

We have worked with logs from the Apache HTTP web server. The reality is that we can apply the same ideals and methodology to any log file. We will take a look at Postfix mail logs. The mail log holds all activity from the SMTP server and we can then see who has been sending e-mails to whom. The log file is usually located at `/var/log/mail.log`. I will access this on my Ubuntu 15.10 server that has a local e-mail delivery. All this means is that the STMP server is listening only to the localhost interface of `127.0.0.1`.

The log format will change a little depending on the type of message. For example, `$7` will contain `from` logs on outbound message, whereas inbound messages will contain `to`.

If we want to list all the inbound messages to the SMTP server, we can use the following command:

```
# awk '  ( $7 ~ /^to/ ) ' /var/log/mail.log
```

As the string `to` is very short, we can add identification to it by ensuring that the field begins with to using the `^`. The command and output is shown in the following screenshot:

```
root@andrew-15-10:~# awk '( $7 ~ /^to/ )' /var/log/mail.log
Oct 12 17:00:47 andrew-15-10 postfix/local[10109]: 80346680E8: to=<root@andrew-15-10>, relay=local, d
elay=0.14, delays=0.09/0.05/0/0.01, dsn=2.0.0, status=sent (delivered to mailbox)
root@andrew-15-10:~# 
```

It will be easy to extend the `to` or `from` searches to also include users names. We can see the format of the delivered or received mail. Working with the same template we used with the Apache logs, we can easily display the highest recipient or sender.

Summary

We now have some heavy ammunition behind our text processing and we can begin to understand just how powerful awk can be. Working with real data is particularly useful in gauging the performance and accuracy of our searches. Having begun working with simple Apache entries on the newly installed Ubuntu 15.10 Apache web server, we soon migrated to the larger sample data from a live web server. With 30,000 lines, this file gives us some real meat to work with and in no time we were able to produce credible reports. We closed up the return to the Ubuntu 15.10 server to analyze the Postfix SMTP logs. We can see that we can very much drag and drop the technology that we have previously used into the new log files.

Next up, we stick with awk and look at how we can report on the lastlog data and on flat XML files.

12
A Better lastlog with Awk

We have already seen in *Chapter 11, Summarizing Logs with Awk,* how we can create complex reports from large amounts of data mined from purely text files. Similarly, we can create extensive reports using the output from standard command-line tools, such as the lastlog tool. In itself lastlog can report the last login time for all users. Often though, we may wish to filter the output from lastlog. Perhaps you need to exclude the user accounts that have never been used to login to the system. It may also be irrelevant to report on root, as the account may be predominately used for sudo only and not used to record regularly for standard logins.

In working through this chapter, we will work both with lastlog and formatting of XML data. As this is the last chapter in which we investigate awk, we will configure record separators. We have already seen the use of field separators in awk but we can change the default record separator from a newline to something more specific to our need. More specifically, within this chapter we will cover:

- Using awk ranges to exclude data
- Conditions based on the number of fields in a row
- Manipulating the awk record separator to report on XML data

Using awk ranges to exclude data

So far in this book, we have predominately looked at including data with ranges either for sed or for awk. With both of these tools, we can negate the range so that we exclude the specified rows. This suits the need that we have been using the output from lastlog. This will print all the login data for all the users, including accounts that have never been logged in. These accounts that have never been logged in might be service accounts or for new users that have not logged into the system so far.

The lastlog command

If we look at the output from `lastlog`, when it is used without any options, we can begin to understand the issue. From the command line, we execute the command as a standard user. There is no requirement to run it as the root account. The command is shown in the following example:

```
$ lastlog
```

The partial output is shown within the following screenshot:

```
gdm                                          **Never logged in**
sshd                                         **Never logged in**
tcpdump                                      **Never logged in**
tux              pts/1      localhost        Tue Oct 20 13:02:35 +0100 2015
bob                                          **Never logged in**
u1                                           **Never logged in**
vboxadd                                      **Never logged in**
```

We can see, even from this limited output that we have a cluttered output due to the virtual noise being created by the accounts that have not logged in. It is possible to alleviate this to some degree using the `lastlog` options but it may not entirely resolve the issue. To demonstrate this, we can add an option to `lastlog` that only users accounts usually used by standard accounts should be included. This may vary on your system but on the sample CentOS 6 host that I am using, the first user will be UID 500.

If we use the `lastlog -u 500-5000` command, we will only print data for those users with a UID within this range. On the simple demonstration system, we have just three user accounts for which the output is acceptable. However, we can understand that we may still have some clutter die to these accounts that have not yet been used. This is shown in the following screenshot:

```
centos6 ~ $ lastlog -u 500-5000
Username         Port       From             Latest
tux              pts/1      localhost        Tue Oct 20 13:02:35 +0100 2015
bob                                          **Never logged in**
u1                                           **Never logged in**
centos6 ~ $ ▋
```

In addition to the superfluous data being printed from the **Never logged in** accounts, we may only be interested in the **Username** and **Latest** fields. This is another reason to support the need to use awk as our data filter. In this way, we can provide both horizontal and vertical data filtering, rows, and columns.

Horizontal filtering rows with awk

To provide this filtering using awk, we will pipe the data from `lastlog` directly to awk. We will make use of a simple control file initially providing the horizontal filtering or reducing the rows that we see. First, the command pipeline will be as simple as the following command example:

```
$ lastlog | awk -f lastlog.awk
```

Of course, the complexity is abstracted from the command line and concealed within the control file that we use. Initially, the control file is kept simple and would read as follows:

```
!(/Never logged in/ || /^Username/ || /^root/) {
  print $0;
}
```

The range is setup as we have seen previously and precedes the main code block. Using the exclamation mark in front of the parentheses negates or reverses the selected range. The double vertical bar acts as a logical OR. We do not include lines that contain `Never logged in`, nor do we include lines that start with `Username`. This removes the header-line that is printed by `lastlog`. Finally, we exclude the root account from the display. This initiates the rows that we work with and the main code block will print those lines.

Counting matched rows

We may also want to count the number of rows that are returned by the filter. For example, using the internal NR variable will show all rows and not just the matched rows; for us to be able to report the number of users that have logged in, we must use our own variable. The following code will maintain the count within the variable that we name cnt. We increment this using the C style ++ for each iteration of the main code block. We can use the END code block to display the closing value of this variable:

```
!(/Never logged in/ || /^Username/ || /^root/) {
  cnt++
  print $0;
}
END {
  print "========================"
  print "Total Number of Users Processed: ", cnt
}
```

We can see from the following code and output how this appears on my system:

```
centos6 ~ $ lastlog | awk -f ll.awk
tux             pts/1    localhost        Tue Oct 20 13:02:35 +0100 2015
=====================
Total Number of Users Processed:   1
centos6 ~ $ █
```

From the display output, we can now see that we show only users that have logged in and in this case, it is just the single user. However, we may also decide that we want to abstract the data further and display only certain fields from the matched rows. This should be a simple task but it is complicated, as the number of fields will vary depending on how the login was executed.

Conditions based on the number of fields

If a user logs onto the server's physical console directly rather than logging on through a remote or graphical pseudo-terminal, then the `lastlog` output will not display the host field. To demonstrate this, I have logged onto my CentOS host directly to the `tty1` console and avoided the GUI. The output from the previous awk control file shows that we now have the users **tux** and **bob**; **bob** though is lacking the host field as he is connected to a console.

```
centos6 ~ $ lastlog | awk -f ll.awk
tux             pts/1    192.168.0.3      Thu Oct 22 13:31:04 +0100 2015
bob             tty1                      Thu Oct 22 13:34:48 +0100 2015
=====================
Total Number of Users Processed:   2
centos6 ~ $ █
```

Although in itself it's not an issue but it will be if we want to filter the fields and the two row's field numbers will vary where a field is omitted from some lines. For `lastlog` we will have 9 fields for most connections and only 8 fields for those that connect directly to the server console. The desire for the application is that we print the username and the date, but not the time of the last login. We will also print our own header in the `BEGIN` block. To ensure that we use the correct placements we will need to count the fields in each row using the `NF` internal variable.

For the 8 fields lines we want to print fields 1, 4, 5, and 8; for the longer lines with additional host information, we will use fields 1, 5, 6 and 9. We will also use printf so that we can align the column data correctly. The control file should be edited, as shown in the following example:

```
BEGIN {
printf "%8s %11s\n","Username","Login date"
print "===================="
}
!(/Never logged in/ || /^Username/ || /^root/) {
cnt++
if ( NF == 8 )
    printf "%8s %2s %3s %4s\n", $1,$5,$4,$8

else
    printf "%8s %2s %3s %4s\n", $1,$6,$5,$9
}
END {
print "===================="
print "Total Number of Users Processed: ", cnt
}
```

We can see the command and the output it produces in the following screenshot. We can see how we can create a more suitable display based on information that we want to focus on:

```
centos6 ~ $ lastlog | awk -f ll.awk
Username  Login date
====================
     tux 22 Oct 2015
     bob 22 Oct 2015
====================
Total Number of Users Processed:  2
centos6 ~ $ █
```

If we look at the output, I have chosen to display the date before the month so we do not display the fields in the numeric order. This, of course, is a personal choice and customizable to suit the way you feel the data should be displayed.

We can use the principles of what we have seen in the lastlog control file with output from any command and you should practise with the commands that you want to filter the data from.

Manipulating the awk record separator to report on XML data

So far, while we have been working with awk we have limited ourselves to working with individual rows, with each new row representing a new record. Although this is often what we want, where we work with tagged data, such as XML where an individual record may span multiple lines. In this case, we may need to look at setting the RS or record separator internal variable.

Apache Virtual Hosts

In *Chapter 9*, *Automating Apache Virtual Hosts* we worked with **Apache Virtual Hosts**. This uses tagged data that defines the start and end of each Virtual Host. Even though we prefer to store each Virtual Host in their own file, they can be combined into a single file. Consider the following file that stores the possible Virtual Host definitions, this can be stored as the `virtualhost.conf` file, as shown:

```
<VirtualHost *:80>
DocumentRoot /www/example
ServerName www.example.org
# Other directives here
</VirtualHost>

<VirtualHost *:80>
DocumentRoot /www/theurbanpenguin
ServerName www.theurbanpenguin.com
# Other directives here
</VirtualHost>

<VirtualHost *:80>
DocumentRoot /www/packt
ServerName www.packtpub.com
# Other directives here
</VirtualHost>
```

We have the three Virtual Hosts within a single file. Each record is separated by an empty line, meaning that we have two new line characters that logically separate each entry. We will explain this to awk by setting the RS variable as follows: `RS="\n\n"`. With this in place, we can then print the required Virtual Host record. This will be set in the BEGIN code block of the control file.

We will also need to dynamically search the command line for the desired host configuration. We build this into the control file. The control file should look similar to the following code:

```
BEGIN { RS="\n\n" ; }
$0 ~ search { print }
```

The BEGIN block sets the variable and then we move onto the range. The range is set so that the record ($0) matches (~) the search variable. We must set the variable when awk is executed. The following command demonstrates the command line execution where the control file and configuration file are located within our working directory:

```
$ awk -f vh.awk search=packt virtualhost.conf
```

We can see this more clearly by looking at the command and the output that is produced in the following screenshot:

```
centos6 ~ $ awk -f vh.awk search=packt virtualhost.conf
<VirtualHost *:80>
DocumentRoot /www/packt
ServerName www.packtpub.com
# Other directives here
</VirtualHost>
centos6 ~ $ █
```

XML catalog

We can extend this further into XML files where we may not want to display the complete record, but just certain fields. If we consider the following product catalog:

```
<product>
<name>drill</name>
<price>99</price>
<stock>5</stock>
</product>

<product>
<name>hammer</name>
<price>10</price>
<stock>50</stock>
</product>

<product>
<name>screwdriver</name>
```

```
<price>5</price>
<stock>51</stock>
</product>

<product>
<name>table saw</name>
<price>1099.99</price>
<stock>5</stock>
</product>
```

Logically, each record is delimited as before with the empty line. Each field though is a little more detailed and we need to use the delimiter as follows: FS="[><]". We define either the opening or closing angle bracket as the field delimiter.

To help analyze this, we can print a single record as follows:

```
<product><name>top</name><price>9</price><stock>5</stock></product>
```

Each angle brace is a field separator, which means that we will have some empty fields. We could rewrite this line as a CSV file:

```
,product,,name,top,/name,,price,9,/price,,stock,5,/stock,,/product,
```

We just replace each angle bracket with a comma, in this way it is more easily read by us. We can see that the content of field 5 is the top value.

Of course, we will not edit the XML file, we will leave it in the XML format. The conversion here is just to highlight how the field separators can be read.

The control file that we use to extract data from the XML file is illustrated in the following code example:

```
BEGIN { FS="[><]"; RS="\n\n" ; OFS=""; }
$0 ~ search { print $4 ": " $5, $8 ": " $9, $12 ": " $13 }
```

Within the BEGIN code block, we set the FS and RS variables as we have discussed. We also set the OFS or **Output Field Separator** to a space. In this way, when we print the fields we separate the values with a space rather than leaving in the angle brackets. The ranch makes use of the same match as we used before when looking at the Virtual Hosts.

If we need to search for the product drill from within the catalog we can use the command laid out in the following example:

```
$ awk -f catalog.awk search=drill catalog.xml
```

The following screenshot shows the output in detail:

```
centos6 ~ $ awk -f catalog.awk search=drill catalog.xml
name: drill price: 99 stock: 5
centos6 ~ $ ▮
```

We have now been able to take a rather messy XML file and create readable reports from the catalog. The power of awk is highlighted again and for us, the last time within this book. By now, I hope you too can start to make use of this on a regular basis.

Summary

We have had three Chapters where we have used awk. Starting with some basic usage statements in *Chapter 10*, *Awk Fundamentals* where we became comfortable. Within *Chapter 11*, *Summarizing Logs with Awk* and this chapter we started building our bespoke applications.

Specifically, in this chapter we saw how we could create reports from the output of standard commands, such as lastlog. We saw that we could negate ranges and additionally make use of the OR statement. We then built the application that will allow us to query XML data.

For the next two chapters, we will move away from the shell scripts and look at scripts using perl and Python so we can compare the scripting languages and make appropriate choices.

13
Using Perl as a Bash Scripting Alternative

Scripting with bash can help you with the automation of tasks and you can achieve a great deal by mastering bash scripting. However, your journey should not end with bash. While we have seen the power available in your bash scripts, we are limited by the commands we can run and the options they have. Bash scripts allow us to access commands; whereas, if we use Perl scripts, we have access to the programming interfaces or the APIs of the system. In this way, we can often achieve more with fewer resources.

In this chapter, we will introduce Perl scripting and some other basic scripts that we can use to learn Perl; we will cover the following topics:

- What is Perl?
- Hello World
- Arrays in Perl
- Conditional tests in Perl
- Functions

What is Perl?

Perl is a scripting language that was developed in the 1980's by Larry Wall to extend the functionality of sed and awk. It is an acronym for **Practical Extraction and Reporting Language** but has grown far bigger than its original purpose and today it is available on Unix, Linux, OS X, and Windows operating systems.

Although, it is a scripting language, it is not shell scripting; as such there is no Perl shell. This means that the code has to be executed via Perl scripts and not directly from the command line. The exception to this is the -e option to the perl command that can allow you to execute a perl statement. For example, we can use the following command line to print the ubiquitous Hello World:

```
$ perl -e ' print("Hello World\n");'
```

You will find that Perl is installed by default on most Linux and Unix systems as many programs will make use of Perl in their code. To check the version of Perl that you have installed on your system you can use the perl command, as follows:

```
$ perl -v
```

The output of this command is shown in the following screenshot from my Raspberry Pi:

```
pi@pilabs ~ $ perl -v

This is perl 5, version 14, subversion 2 (v5.14.2) built
-thread-multi-64int
(with 89 registered patches, see perl -V for more detail)
```

In this chapter, Perl in uppercase will refer to the language and perl in lowercase will refer to the command.

If we create a Perl script, just like bash it will be an interpreted language and the first line will be the shebang, so that the system knows which command is to be used to read the script. The /usr/bin/perl command can be used to locate perl often. To verify this, you may use:

```
$ which perl
```

Unlike bash, when the perl command reads the script it will optimize the script at runtime; one simple feature that this will enable is that we can define the functions at the end of the script, rather than before they are used. We will see this as we look at the Perl script in more detail, as we work through this chapter.

Hello World

To create a simple Perl script, we can use the text editor of choice. For short scripts vi or vim works well, as does gedit if you want to work in GUI. For larger projects an IDE may help. Often, the IDE will allow you to change the object name easily throughout the script and provide expansion of object names. In this chapter, we will make use of very simple scripts so we will continue to use vi.

We will create a $HOME/bin/hello.pl file to produce the output we want:

```
#!/usr/bin/perl
print("Hello World\n");
```

The file still needs to be in a directory within our PATH variable; hence, we create $HOME/bin. If it is not in the PATH variable then we will need to specify the full or relative path of the file, as with bash.

The file will need to be set with the execute permission. We can do this with the following command:

$ chmod u+x $HOME/bin/hello.pl

We can run the script with the following command:

$ hello.pl

We can see that the code that we have added is the same as the one we ran the earlier perl -e command with. The only difference is the shebang. This is also quite similar to bash. We now use the print function rather than using the echo command. Bash scripts run a series of commands, whereas Perl scripts run functions. The print function does not automatically add a new line so we add it ourselves using the \n character. We can also see that the Perl uses the semi-colon to terminate a line of code. The shebang is not a line of code, whereas the print line is terminated with a semicolon.

If we are using Perl version 5.10 or later, on the Pi we have seen that it is 5.14 and we can also make use of a function say. Similar to the print command, this is used to display output but it also includes the newline. We have to enable this feature, which is managed by the use keyword. Either of the following scripts will print Hello World using the say function:

```
#!/usr/bin/perl
use v5.10;
say("Hello World");
```

```
#!/usr/bin/perl
use 5.10.0;
say("Hello World");
```

The say function also simplifies the printing of files and lists.

Perl arrays

Something that we can make use of in Perl is an array. These arrays are variables that are created from lists; put simply, they are basically multi-valued variables. If we were to use a container analogy to describe a variable, it will be either a cup or a placeholder for one value. An array will be analogous to a crate. We can describe the crate with a single name but we have to include additional naming elements to access each slot within the crate. A crate can hold more than a single item, just like an array.

We saw that by using bash scripting we can pass command line arguments in the script. The arguments were using their own variable name, $1, $2, and so on. This also clashed with the name of the program, to a degree, because of the fact that it was $0. Even though they may appear similar, there is no logical relationship between $0 and $1. The $0 variable is the name of the script and $1 is the first argument. When we look at this in Perl, we can start to see some of the major differences.

Program name?

The program name in Perl can still be accessed with the $0 variable. We can see this in the following script:

```
#!/usr/bin/perl
print("You are using $0\n");
print("Hello World\n");
```

Now, even though we think of $0 as quite simple to use, as we have accessed it in bash before, if we approach this with fresh eyes it is not so obvious. Perl has a module called English where we have some more friendly names defined for many other variables used in Perl. If we take a look at the following script we can see this in use:

```
#!/usr/bin/perl
use English;
print("You are using $PROGRAM_NAME\n");
print("Hello World\n");
```

The line `use English;` will import the module that redefines `$0` so that it can be referenced as `$PROGRAM_NAME`. Although, this requires more typing it also acts as a better name documenting its purpose.

Argument arrays

Rather than using `$1`, `$2`, and so on for the arguments; Perl now uses a list of arguments stored in a single array variable. The array name is `@ARGV` and we can access each argument supplied by this in the index number or slot number. The computers start counting at `0`, so the first argument will be `$ARGV[0]`, the second will be `$ARGV[1]`, and so on.

 An index array is named using the @ symbol. Each element of the array is still a single or scalar variable and just like in bash, they are read with the $ symbol.

When we look at the following script, `$HOME/bin/args.pl`, we can see how to make the Hello script more portable by accepting arguments:

```
#!/usr/bin/perl
use English;
print("You are using $PROGRAM_NAME\n");
print("Hello $ARGV[0]\n");
```

We can see this in action by running the script, as shown in the following screenshot:

```
pi@pilabs ~/bin $ ./args.pl fred
You are using ./args.pl
Hello fred
pi@pilabs ~/bin $ _
```

Counting elements in an array

We can see that the command-line arguments are stored in the `@ARGV` array. We can count the number of arguments or, in fact, the elements in any array using the following code:

```
scalar @<array-name>;
```

So instead of using the `$#` to count the supplied arguments, we will use the code as follows:

```
scalar @ARGV;
```

If we add this to our script, it will be seen, as shown in the following code block:

```
#!/usr/bin/perl
use English;
print("You are using $PROGRAM_NAME\n");
print("You have supplied: " . scalar @ARGV . " arguments\n");
print("Hello $ARGV[0]\n");
```

 We can also take a note from the previous code block that we can concatenate the output of a command with a test using the period character.

Looping through an array

In bash, we have a simple mechanism with `$*` to refer the list of arguments supplied to a script. In Perl, this is just a little different from having to loop through the list. However, the `foreach` keyword is built for this:

```
#!/usr/bin/perl
use English;
print("You are using $PROGRAM_NAME\n");
print("You have supplied " . scalar @ARGV . " arguments\n");
foreach $arg (@ARGV) {
 print("Hello $arg\n");
}
```

We can see that the code is defined within the loop and is contained using the brace brackets. If you recall, bash did not specifically have a `foreach` keyword and it made use of do and done to constrain the code.

If we implement this code in the `$HOME/bin/forargs.pl` file, we can execute it as a code similar to the following screenshot:

```
pi@pilabs ~/bin $ ./forargs.pl   fred bob
You are using ./forargs.pl
You have supplied 2 arguments
Hello fred
Hello bob
pi@pilabs ~/bin $
```

Creating arrays

So far, we have relied on the `@ARGV` system array and this has proved to be a great way to learn how to access and array. We now need to see how to create arrays of our own design.

Arrays are lists of values that can store mixed data types; so, there is no reason why we cannot have an array that stores both strings and numbers. The order in which the items are supplied to the array will set their index position. In other words, the first item in the list will be the first index or index `0` in the array. Consider the following code: `$HOME/bin/array.pl`:

```perl
#!/usr/bin/perl
use English;
print("You are using $PROGRAM_NAME\n");
@user = ("Fred","Bloggs",24);
print("$user[0] $user[1] is @user[2]\n");
```

The first thing we should notice is that when we are setting a variable of any type, including an array, we will use the designator for the variable type. We see here that the use of `@user = ...`, will make use of the `@` symbol as previously mentioned to denote that the variable is an array variable. If we were setting a scalar variable similar to the ones we use in bash, we will set `$user`. In bash, we do not use the designator when setting a variable and we cannot have spaces surrounding the assignment operator, `=`. Perl will allow the spaces and aids in the readability with an extra whitespace.

Next, we should notice that the list contains strings and an integer. This is perfectly acceptable and the array can hold different data types. A single name of the array makes sense, as we can now store related data into one object.

The final point to take note of in the supplied code is that we can easily concatenate the string values with integer values using Perl. There is no need to provide any form of data translation. Within the single string, we print the first name, last name, and age of the user.

On script execution, we should receive an output, as shown in the following screenshot:

```
pi@pilabs ~/bin $ ./array.pl
You are using ./array.pl
Fred Bloggs is 24
pi@pilabs ~/bin $
```

Conditional statements in Perl

Similar to the rest of the Perl language, we will have similarities with bash scripting and some completely new ways of implementing conditions. This will often work in our favor; thus, making the code more readable.

Replacing command line lists

First, we do not have the command line list logic, which we use in bash and we do not make use of the && and ||. Instead of these rather weird looking symbols, the conditional logic for single statements in Perl is written in the following manner:

```
exit(2) if scalar @ARGV < 1;
print("Hello $ARGV[0]\n") unless scalar @ARGV == 0;
```

In the first example, we exit with an error code of 2, if we have supplied less than one command-line argument. The bash equivalent to this will be:

```
[ $# -lt 1 ] && exit 2
```

In the second example, we will only print the hello statement if we have supplied arguments. This will be written in bash, as shown in the following example:

```
[ $# -eq 0 ] || echo "Hello $1"
```

Personally, I like Perl; the way as it at least uses words, so we may understand what is happening even if we have not come across the symbols before.

If and unless

Within Perl, as we have already seen in the previous examples, we can make use of negative logic using unless. We both have the traditional if keyword and now unless is an addition. We can use these in our short code, as we have seen or in complete blocks of code.

We can edit the existing args.pl to create a new file: $HOME/bin/ifargs.pl. The file should read similar to the following code:

```perl
#!/usr/bin/perl
use English;
print("You are using $PROGRAM_NAME\n");
my $count = scalar @ARGV;
if ($count > 0) {
  print("You have supplied $count arguments\n");
  print("Hello $ARGV[0]\n");
}
```

The code now has an additional argument, which we have declared and set with the line that reads my $count = scalar @ARGV;. We used this value as a condition for the if statement. The block of code constrained in the brace brackets will execute only if the condition is true.

We demonstrate the running of this program with and without arguments in the following screenshot:

```
pi@pilabs ~/bin $ ./ifargs.pl
You are using ./ifargs.pl
pi@pilabs ~/bin $ ./ifargs.pl fred
You are using ./ifargs.pl
You have supplied 1 arguments
Hello fred
pi@pilabs ~/bin $ _
```

We can write a similar code using unless:

```perl
print("You are using $PROGRAM_NAME\n");
my $count = scalar @ARGV;
unless ($count == 0) {
  print("You have supplied $count arguments\n");
  print("Hello $ARGV[0]\n");

}
```

The code in the brackets now runs only if the condition is false. In this case, if we have not supplied arguments, the code will not run.

Using functions within Perl

As with all languages, the ability to encapsulate a code within functions can make the code more readable and ultimately results in easier to manage codes, with less number of lines. Unlike bash, the functions in Perl can be defined after they are referenced in the code and we often choose to define the functions at the end of the script.

Prompt for user input

We have seen the use of command-line arguments in Perl; now, let's take a look at prompting for user input. This becomes a great way to encapsulate the code to execute and store the prompt within a function. First of all, we will look at a simple script that prompts for the username and then we will modify it to include the function. We will create the $HOME/bin/prompt.pl file to read, as shown in the following code example:

```
#!/usr/bin/perl
my $name;
print("Enter your name: ");
chomp( $name = <STDIN> );
print("Hello $name\n");
```

In line 2, we have declared the variable using my. The keyword my defines the variable with a local scope. In other words, it is local to the block of code that it is created within. As this has been created in the main body of the script, the variable is available to the entire script. The line declares the variable but we do not set the value at this time. Perl does not force you to declare the variables, but it is a good idea and a great practice. In fact, we can tell Perl to enforce this with the use of the use strict; line. We can implement this, as shown in the following code block:

```
#!/usr/bin/perl
use strict;
my $name;
print("Enter your name: ");
chomp( $name = <STDIN> );
print("Hello $name\n");
```

With this in place, we are forced to declare the variables and the code will fail if they are not. The idea behind this is to help troubleshooting by identifying misspelled variables later in the code. Try deleting the line starting with my and re-executing the code; it will fail. Similarly, we can make use of the use warnings; line, to warn us if we have used a variable only once.

We prompt for the user name and do not use a newline here. We want the prompt to be on the same line with the one the user will enter the data into. The function chomp is great isn't it? This function will remove or chomp the newline from the input that we submit. We will need to use the *Enter* key to submit the data and chomp removes the newline for us.

Creating the function

We are currently only prompting for a user name, so we need just one prompt but we could easily ask for a first name and last name. Rather than writing the code for the prompt each time, we can create a function. These are defined using the keyword sub, as we can see in the following code:

```
#!/usr/bin/perl
use strict;
my $name = prompt_user("Enter a name: ");
print("Hello $name\n");

sub prompt_user () {
    my $n;
    print($_[0]);
    chomp( $n = <STDIN> );
    return($n);
}
```

The prompt_user function takes a single argument, which will become the message to display with the prompt. For the reference to the argument, we use the system array @_ and index 0. This is written as $_[0]. If we remember, arrays are multi-valued and each entry in the array is a scalar variable. Within the function, we use the function return to send the value that the user has set back to the calling code. We can see that the main code block is simpler now with the code for the prompt being abstracted into a function. When we look at this, we may think that it took a lot of work, but when we look at adding it in a prompt for a first name and last name, it is now much simpler.

Functions are good things to use and hopefully the following code will help you see this:

```perl
#!/usr/bin/perl
use strict;
my $fname = prompt_user("Enter a first name: ");
my $lname = prompt_user("Enter a last name: ");

print("Hello $fname $lname\n");

sub prompt_user () {
    my $n;
    print($_[0]);
    chomp( $n = <STDIN> );
    return($n);
}
```

Summary

So this concludes our whirlwind tour and the introduction to Perl. We have seen the similarities with bash, as well as, the new features and differences. The main points to take from this are that once you become proficient in one language it becomes easier to learn other coding languages.

To keep us in the mood of learning new languages, we will now take a quick tour of Python in the next chapter.

14
Using Python as a Bash Scripting Alternative

Python is another scripting language and the newest that we have looked at so far. Similar to bash and Perl, Python is an interpreted language and makes use of the shebang. Although, it does not have a shell interface, we can access a console called the REPL where we can type Python codes to interact with the system. In this chapter we will cover the following topics:

- What is Python?
- Saying Hello the Python way
- Pythonic arguments
- Significant whitespace
- Read user input
- Using Python to write to files

What is Python?

Python is an object-oriented interpreted language that is designed to be easy to use and to aid Rapid Application Development. This is achieved by the use of simplified semantics in the language.

Python was born at the end of the 1980's, towards the very end of December 1989 by the Dutch developer, Guido van Rossum. A majority of the design of the language is aimed at clarity and simplicity and one of the main rules of the *Zen of Python* is:

"There should be one, and preferable only one, obvious way to do it."

Often systems will have both Python 2 and Python 3 installed; however, all newer distributions are switching to Python 3. We will be working with Python 3, it being the latest version installed on the Raspberry Pi.

Although, there is no shell, we can interact with Python using REPL: read, evaluate, print, and loop. We can access this by typing python3 in the command line. You should see something similar to the following screenshot:

```
pi@pilabs ~/bin $ python3
Python 3.2.3 (default, Mar  1 2013, 11:53:50)
[GCC 4.6.3] on linux2
Type "help", "copyright", "credits" or "license" for more information.
>>>
```

We can see that we are presented with the **>>>** prompt and this is known as the REPL console. We should emphasize that this is a scripting language and like bash and Perl, we will normally execute a code through the text files that we create. Those text files will normally be expected to have a .py suffix to their name.

While working with REPL, we can print the version independently by importing a module. In Perl, we will use the keyword, in bash we will use the command source and in Python we use import:

>>>import sys

With the module loaded, we can now investigate the object-oriented nature of Python by printing the version:

>>> sys.version

We will navigate to the sys object within our namespace and call the version method from that object.

Combining these two commands together, we should be able to see the following output:

```
>>> import sys
>>> sys.version
'3.2.3 (default, Mar  1 2013, 11:53:50) \n[GCC 4.6.3]'
>>>
```

To close this section about describing Python, we should take a look at the
Zen of Python. From REPL, we can type `import this`, as shown in the
following screenshot:

```
>>> import this
The Zen of Python, by Tim Peters

Beautiful is better than ugly.
Explicit is better than implicit.
Simple is better than complex.
Complex is better than complicated.
Flat is better than nested.
Sparse is better than dense.
Readability counts.
Special cases aren't special enough to break the rules.
Although practicality beats purity.
Errors should never pass silently.
Unless explicitly silenced.
In the face of ambiguity, refuse the temptation to guess.
There should be one-- and preferably only one --obvious way to do it.
Although that way may not be obvious at first unless you're Dutch.
Now is better than never.
Although never is often better than *right* now.
If the implementation is hard to explain, it's a bad idea.
If the implementation is easy to explain, it may be a good idea.
Namespaces are one honking great idea -- let's do more of those!
>>>
```

This is far more than just the Zen of Python; it actually makes up a good rule for all
programming languages and a guide for developers.

Finally, to close the REPL, we will use *Ctrl + d* in Linux or *Ctrl + z* in Windows.

Saying Hello World the Python way

The code we write in Python should be clear and uncluttered, sparse is better than
dense. We will need the shebang on the first line and then the `print` statement.
The `print` function includes the newline and we do not need semicolons at the
end of the line. We can see the edited version of `$HOME/bin/hello.py` in the
following example:

```
#!/usr/bin/python3
print("Hello World")
```

We will still need to add the execute permission, but we can run the code as earlier using chmod. This shown in the following command but we should be a little used to this now:

```
$ chmod u+x $HOME/bin/hello.py
```

Finally, we can now execute the code to see our greeting.

Again, knowing at least one language makes it easier to adapt to others and there is not a lot of new features in this.

Pythonic arguments

We should know by now that we will want to be able to pass command-line arguments to Python and we can do this using the argv array similar to Perl. However, we are more like bash, with Python we combine the program name into the array with the other arguments. Python also uses lowercase instead of uppercase in the object name.

- The argv array is a part of the sys object
- sys.argv[0] is the script name
- sys.argv[1] is the first argument supplied to the script
- sys.argv[2] is the second supplied argument and so on
- The argument count will always be at least 1, so, keep this in mind when checking for supplied arguments

Supplying arguments

If we create the $HOME/bin/args.py file we can see this in action. The file should be created as follows and made executable:

```
#!/usr/bin/python3
import sys
print("Hello " + sys.argv[1])
```

If we run the script with a supplied argument, we should be able to see something similar to the following screenshot:

```
pi@pilabs ~/bin $ ./args.py fred
Hello fred
pi@pilabs ~/bin $ _
```

Our code is still quite clean and simple; however, we may have noticed that we cannot combine the quoted text in the `print` statement with the argument. We use the + symbol to join or concatenate the two strings together. As there is no specific symbol to denote a variable or any other type of object, they cannot appear as a static text within quotes.

Counting arguments

As it was previously mentioned, the script name is the first argument at index 0 of the array. So, if we try to count the arguments, then the count should always be at the very least one In other words, if we have not supplied arguments, the argument count will be one. To count the items in an array, we can use the `len()` function. If we edit the script to include a new line we will see this work, as follows:

```
#!/usr/bin/python3
import sys
print("Hello " + sys.argv[1])
print( len(sys.argv) )
```

Executing the code as we have earlier, we can see that we have supplied two arguments. The script name and then the string `fred`:

```
pi@pilabs ~/bin $ ./args.py fred
Hello fred
2
pi@pilabs ~/bin $
```

If we try and have a single `print` statement to print the output and the number of arguments, then we will find that Python does not like mixing data types. The length value is an integer and this cannot be mixed with strings without conversion. The following code will fail:

```
#!/usr/bin/python3
import sys
print("Hello " + sys.argv[1] + " " + len(sys.argv))
```

However, this is not a mammoth task and just requires an explicit conversion. From the Zen of Python:

"Explicit is better than implicit."

The code will work if modified, as follows:

```
#!/usr/bin/python3
import sys
print("Hello " + sys.argv[1] + " " + str(len(sys.argv)))
```

If we try to run the script and omit to supply an argument, then there will be a null value in the array when we reference index 1. This will give an error, as shown in the following screenshot:

```
pi@pilabs ~/bin $ ./args.py
Traceback (most recent call last):
  File "./args.py", line 3, in <module>
    print("Hello " + sys.argv[1] + " " + str(len(sys.argv)))
IndexError: list index out of range
pi@pilabs ~/bin $ _
```

We of course need to handle this to prevent the error and we can now pass into the section of significant whitespace.

Significant whitespace

A major difference between Python and most other languages is that additional whitespace can mean something. The indent level of your code defines the block of code to which it belongs. So far, we have not indented the code we have created past the start of the line. This means that all of the code is at the same indent level and belongs to the same code block. Rather than using brace brackets or do and done keywords to define the code block, we use indents. If we indent with four spaces, then we must stick to those four spaces. When we return to the previous indent level, we return to the previous code block.

This seems complex but it is really quite simple and keeps your code clean and uncluttered. If we edit the arg.py file to prevent unwelcomed errors, if an argument is not supplied, we can see this in action:

```
#!/usr/bin/python3
import sys
count = len(sys.argv)
if ( count > 1 ):
    print("Arguments supplied: " + str(count))
    print("Hello " + sys.argv[1])
print("Exiting " + sys.argv[0])
```

The `if` statement checks if the argument count is greater than 1 or not. We now store for ease, the argument count has its own variable, which we call `count`. The code block starts with the colon and then all of the following code that is indented to four spaces is part of the code that will execute when the condition returns to true.

When we return to the previous indent level, we return to the main code block and we execute the code regardless of the status of the condition.

We can see this illustrated in the following screenshot, where we can execute the script with and without the argument:

```
pi@pilabs ~/bin $ ./args.py
Exiting ./args.py
pi@pilabs ~/bin $ ./args.py fred
Arguments supplied: 2
Hello fred
Exiting ./args.py
```

Reading user input

If we want the welcome message to greet us by name no matter whether we supply the argument to the script or not, we can add in a prompt to capture the data while the script is running. Python makes this simple and easy to implement. We can see from the edited file shown in the screenshot that follows how this is achieved:

```python
#!/usr/bin/python3
import sys
count = len(sys.argv)
name = ''

if ( count == 1 ):
    name = input("Enter a name: ")
else:
    name = sys.argv[1]

print("Hello " + name)
print("Exiting " + sys.argv[0])
```

We make use of a new variable in the script that we set in the main block initially, to be an empty string. Set it here to make the variable available to the complete script and all code blocks.

The `input` function in Python 3 or `raw_input` can be used in Python 2 to gain user input. We store that input in the `name` variable. If we have supplied an argument we pick it up on the code in the `else` block and set the `name` variable to the first supplied argument. It is this that is used in the `print` statement back in the main block.

Using Python to write to files

To add some variety to this chapter, we will now look at printing this data to a file. Again using Python, this is quite a simple and easy way to pick up. We will start by making a copy of our existing `args.py`. We will copy this to `$HOME/bin/file.py`. The new `file.py` should read similar to the following screenshot and have the execute permission set:

```python
#!/usr/bin/python3
import sys
count = len(sys.argv)
name = ''

if ( count == 1 ):
    name = input("Enter a name: ")
else:
    name = sys.argv[1]

log = open("/tmp/script.log","a")
log.write("Hello " + name + "\n")
log.close()
```

You will notice that we have just altered the final lines and instead of print we now open a file. We also see more of the object-orientated life of Python that dynamically assigns the `write()` and `close()` methods to the object log, as it is seen as an instance of a file. When we open the file, we open it up for the purpose of appending, meaning that we do not overwrite the existing content if it is already there. If the file is not there, we will create a new file. If we use `w`, we will open the file for writing, which might translate to overwriting, so take care.

You can see that this is an easy task and this is why Python is used in many applications and is taught widely in schools.

Summary

This now finishes our look at Python and it certainly has been a brief tour. We can again emphasize the similarities that you will see in many languages and the importance of learning any coding language. What you learn in one language will help in most of the other languages that you come across.

What we learn from the Zen of Python will help us design and develop a great code. We can print the Zen of Python using the following Python code:

```
>>>import this
```

We can type the code on the REPL prompt. Keeping your code clean and well-spaced out will aid in the readability and ultimately this will help with the maintenance of the code.

We have also seen that the Python likes you to be explicit in your code and will not implicitly convert the data types.

We are also at the end of the book but hopefully, the start of your scripting career. Good luck and thank you for reading.

Index

Symbol

404 errors
summarizing 133

A

abbreviations
about 45
using 46
advanced test
double [[bracket used 59
Apache name based Virtual Hosts
about 108
creating 108
Apache name based Virtual Hosts templates
creating 109
creating, steps 109
lines, isolating 110, 111
sed script files 111-113
Apache Virtual Hosts 144, 145
argument identifier 12
arguments, Python
about 164
counting 165, 166
supplying 164, 165
arithmetic operations, double ((brackets used
about 61
parameter manipulation 62
simple math 61
standard arithmetic tests 63
arrays, Perl
about 152
argument arrays 153
creating 155
elements, counting 153
looping through 154
program name, accessing 152
awk command
history 121
awk control file
about 128
example 128
awk ranges
for excluding data 139
lastlog command 140
matched rows, counting 141, 142
rows, horizontal filtering 141
awk record separator, manipulating
Apache Virtual Hosts 144, 145
for reporting on XML data 144
XML catalog 145-147

B

backup2.sh
creating, with elif keyword 37
bash
about 1
vulnerabilities 1-3
bash command hierarchy
about 3
command PATH 5
command type 3, 4
basic script
creating, with read command 21
browser data
displaying 136, 137

C

case statements
  using 39, 40
code snippets
  colors, providing for message
      interpretation 47-49
  using 46, 47
command
  types 3
command-line lists
  used, for simple decision paths 29, 30
  used, for verifying user input 31
conditional statement, Perl
  about 156
  command line lists, replacing 156
  if keyword 157
  unless keyword 157, 158
conditional statements
  creating, with if statement 34-36
**conditions, based on number
      of fields 142, 143**
content
  displaying, from files 122-124
  filtering, from files 122-124
CPUs
  listing, in system 94-97
CSV files
  about 97
  catalog entries, isolating 100
  parsing 97-99

D

data
  displaying, from web logs 131
double [[bracket
  advanced features 59
  pattern matching 59
  regular expression script 60
  regular expressions 60
  using 59
  whitespace 59

E

echo command
  using, with options 19, 20
elif keyword
  used, for creating backup2.sh 37, 38
  using 37
else keyword
  used, for extending if condition 36
e-mail logs
  working with 137
entered text visibility
  controlling 24
entries
  selecting, by date 131, 132

F

files
  content, displaying 122-124
  content, filtering 122-124
  input, reading 71-73
  testing 52
  writing, with Python 168
file types
  testing 34
for loops
  about 65- 68
  executing 66
front-end
  building, with grep command 41, 42
functions
  about 79-82
  creating 159
  parameters, passing to 82-84
  prompting, for user input 158
  using, in menus 87, 88
  using, with Perl 158
  values, returning from 86

G

gedit
  configuring 7, 8
grep command
  used, for building front-end 41, 42
  used, for displaying text 92

H

Hello Dolly!
about 11
correct quotes, importance 13
script, running with arguments 12, 13
Hello World, Python
writing 163, 164
Hello World! script 9
Hello World script, Perl
creating 151
highest ranking IP address
displaying 135, 136
HTTP access codes
summarizing 133, 134
HTTPD log file format
about 129-131
fields 130

I

if condition
extending, with else keyword 36
if statement
used, for creating conditional
statements 34-36
input
reading, from files 71-73
integers
testing 33
**Integrated Development Environments
(IDEs) 45**
interface
received data, displaying 92

L

lines
isolating 110, 111
logic
adding 52
loop
controlling 69, 70
until loops 70, 71
while loops 70, 71

M

menus
functions, using 87, 88
MySQL/MariaDB database server 27, 28

N

named elements 79
nano
configuring 6
number of entered characters
limiting 23

O

operator menus
creating 74-76
options, vim configuration
autoindent 6
expandtab 6
nohlsearch 6
showmode 6
syntax on 6
tabstop=4 6
output
formatting 125, 126

P

parameter defaults
providing 53
setting 55, 56
special parameters 54
variables 54
parameter expansion 56
parameters
passing, to functions 82-85
quoting 56-58
Perl
about 149, 150
arrays 152
conditional statement 156
functions, using with 158
script, creating 151
ping command 26, 27

Thank you for buying
Mastering Linux Shell Scripting

About Packt Publishing

Packt, pronounced 'packed', published its first book, *Mastering phpMyAdmin for Effective MySQL Management*, in April 2004, and subsequently continued to specialize in publishing highly focused books on specific technologies and solutions.

Our books and publications share the experiences of your fellow IT professionals in adapting and customizing today's systems, applications, and frameworks. Our solution-based books give you the knowledge and power to customize the software and technologies you're using to get the job done. Packt books are more specific and less general than the IT books you have seen in the past. Our unique business model allows us to bring you more focused information, giving you more of what you need to know, and less of what you don't.

Packt is a modern yet unique publishing company that focuses on producing quality, cutting-edge books for communities of developers, administrators, and newbies alike. For more information, please visit our website at www.packtpub.com.

About Packt Open Source

In 2010, Packt launched two new brands, Packt Open Source and Packt Enterprise, in order to continue its focus on specialization. This book is part of the Packt Open Source brand, home to books published on software built around open source licenses, and offering information to anybody from advanced developers to budding web designers. The Open Source brand also runs Packt's Open Source Royalty Scheme, by which Packt gives a royalty to each open source project about whose software a book is sold.

Writing for Packt

We welcome all inquiries from people who are interested in authoring. Book proposals should be sent to author@packtpub.com. If your book idea is still at an early stage and you would like to discuss it first before writing a formal book proposal, then please contact us; one of our commissioning editors will get in touch with you.

We're not just looking for published authors; if you have strong technical skills but no writing experience, our experienced editors can help you develop a writing career, or simply get some additional reward for your expertise.

Linux Shell Scripting Cookbook,
Second Edition

ISBN: 978-1-78216-274-2   Paperback: 384 pages

Over 110 practical recipes to solve real-world shell problems, guaranteed to make you wonder how you ever lived without them

1.   Master the art of crafting one-liner command sequence to perform text processing, digging data from files, backups to sysadmin tools, and a lot more.

2.   And if powerful text processing isn't enough, see how to make your scripts interact with the web-services like Twitter, Gmail.

Scalix: Linux Administrator's Guide

ISBN: 978-1-84719-276-9   Paperback: 276 pages

Install, configure, and administer your Scalix Collaboration Platform email and groupware server

1.   Install, upgrade, and configure Scalix.

2.   Build a robust and reliable system.

3.   Detailed walkthroughs and expert advice on best practices.

Please check **www.PacktPub.com** for information on our titles

[PACKT] open source *
PUBLISHING   community experience distilled

Linux Shell Scripting Cookbook

Linux Shell
Scripting Cookbook

Sarath Lakshman

Linux Shell Scripting Cookbook

ISBN: 978-1-84951-376-0   Paperback: 360 pages

Solve real-world shell scripting problems with over 110 simple but incredibly effective recipes

1. Master the art of crafting one-liner command sequence to perform tasks such as text processing, digging data from files, and lot more.

2. Practical problem solving techniques adherent to the latest Linux platform.

3. Packed with easy-to-follow examples to exercise all the features of the Linux shell scripting language.

Linux Utilities Cookbook

Linux Utilities
Cookbook

James Kent Lewis

Linux Utilities Cookbook

ISBN: 978-1-78216-300-8   Paperback: 224 pages

Over 70 recipes to help you accomplish a wide variety of tasks in Linux quickly and effeciently

1. Use the command line like a pro.

2. Pick a suitable desktop environment.

3. Learn to use files and directories efficiently.

Please check **www.PacktPub.com** for information on our titles

Made in the USA
Middletown, DE
05 May 2018